Walking in Favor
– STEPPING INTO GRACE –

DEVOTIONAL POETRY BY
Sharon Swain

Kingdom Winds
PUBLISHING

Copyright © 2023 by Sharon Swain

All rights reserved. No part of this publication may be reproduced, distributed, or transmitted in any form or by any means, including photocopying, recording, or other electronic or mechanical methods, without the prior written permission of the publisher, except in the case of brief quotations embodied in critical reviews and certain other noncommercial uses permitted by copyright law. For permission requests, write to the publisher at **publishing@kingdomwinds.com**.

Scripture quotations marked NIV are taken from the Holy Bible, New International Version®, NIV® Copyright © 1973, 1978, 1984, 2011 by Biblica, Inc.® Used by permission. All rights reserved worldwide.

Scripture quotations marked ESV are taken from the ESV® Bible (The Holy Bible, English Standard Version®). ESV® Text Edition: 2016. Copyright © 2001 by Crossway, a publishing ministry of Good News Publishers. The ESV® text has been reproduced in cooperation with and by permission of Good News Publishers. Unauthorized reproduction of this publication is prohibited. All rights reserved.

Scripture quotations marked NLT are taken from the Holy Bible, New Living Translation, copyright © 1996, 2004, 2015 by Tyndale House Foundation. Used by permission of Tyndale House Publishers, Inc., Carol Stream, Illinois 60188. All rights reserved.

Scripture quotations marked NASB20 are taken from the New American Standard Bible®, Copyright © 1960, 1971, 1977, 1995, 2020 by The Lockman Foundation. All rights reserved.

Scripture quotations marked TPT are from The Passion Translation®. Copyright © 2017, 2018, 2020 by Passion & Fire Ministries, Inc. Used by permission. All rights reserved. ThePassionTranslation.com.

First Edition, 2023
ISBN 978-1-64590-045-0
Published by Kingdom Winds Publishing.
www.kingdomwinds.com
publishing@kingdomwinds.com

Printed in the United States of America.

DEDICATION

With so much love and joy, I dedicate this book to our four grandchildren: Margo, Harper, Cooper, and Cory. May each one of you come to know and experience the incredible favor and grace of Jesus upon your lives now and for every one of your days!

> "But grow in the grace and knowledge of our Lord and Savior Jesus Christ. To Him be the glory both now and forever! Amen." 2 Peter 3:18 (NIV)

TABLE OF CONTENTS

Dedication	3
Endorsements	8
Foreword	11
Introduction	12
Your Journey in Jesus	14
"Walking in Favor"	18
"Stepping Into Grace"	20

HIS PEACE   26

A Brand New Day	28
A New Lens	30
A Time To Mourn	32
All My Tomorrows	34
An Inner Invitation	36
An Original	38
Bridging the Gap	40
Come to Jesus	42
Empty Spaces	44
Even Though	46
He'll Lead You Home	48
Hide Me Away	50
I've Chosen You	52
Imaginary Cages	54
It's Time	56
Lift Your Load	58
My Called-Out One	60
New Life In Him	62
Once And For All	64
Open Door Policy	66
Rest In Me	68
Sitting with the Master	70
That Still, Small Voice	72
That Stony Heart	74
Union Station	76
Valleys Below	78
Walkin' and All Wobbly	80

Walking in the Valley	82
Walking with Jesus	84
You are Redeemed	86
You'll Be Ok	88
Your Troubled Heart	90

HIS POWER 93

Anointed One	96
A Heart of Worship	98
A One-Man Act	100
Abandoned to You	102
Building Faith	104
Courage Comes From You	106
From Carpenter to King	108
His Precious Blood	110
I'm Calling You	112
Light and Life	114
Out Amongst the Wolves	116
Step Out In The Light	118
The Time Is Now	120
Trust His Steps	122
Walk in His Plan	124
Wrapped in Righteousness	126
Wrapped in Scandal	128
You Will See	130

HIS PRAISE 133

Enamored by Love	136
God With Us	138
Join the Choir	140
My Hope and Rest	142
My Time	144
Our Voices Raised	146
You Are Enough	148
You're My Song	150

HIS PRESENCE — 153

- A Blazing Surrender — 156
- A Spittin' Image — 158
- Blended Lives — 160
- Dynamic Duo — 162
- Enjoying His Presence — 164
- Guard Your Heart — 166
- He Satisfies — 168
- Highly Favored — 170
- Joined to Jesus — 172
- Left Behind — 174
- Nail-Scarred Hands — 176
- Placed in Grace — 178
- Pulling Back the Curtain — 180
- Rekindle Anew — 182
- Steppin' Out And Steppin' In — 184
- The Hour is Late — 186
- Traditions of Men — 188
- Two For One — 190
- Walking in Favor — 192
- Walking in Him — 194
- Walking Through the Cross Today — 196
- Your Yesterdays — 198

HIS PURPOSE — 201

- A Delicious Dish — 204
- Distractions — 206

A Fork In the Road	208
A House Call	210
A Waiting Faith	212
Are You Willing?	214
Come Go With Me	216
Crucified With Christ	218
Divinely Placed	220
Do Not Lose Heart	222
Get in the Game	224
Harvest Time	226
Higher Things	228
Letting Go	230
Listen Up	232
My Glory Days	234
Remember	236
Silent Seasons	238
Sunday's Comin'	240
The Sting of Death	242
This One Thing	244
Time To Let Go	246
Two Contrasting Kingdoms	248
Until Then	250
Washing Dirty Feet	252
Your Calling Is Calling	254
Your Inheritance	256
Acknowledgements	260

ENDORSEMENTS

There is a precious anointing found within the lyrics of Sharon's heartfelt poems. Years spent in intimate relationship with Jesus have formed a sanctuary of love in her heart from which her song is sung. She has stepped into her destiny to be a messenger of His love, healing, and restoration to those desperate to know they are seen and heard by the One who matters most. I am quite sure David wrote Psalm 45:1 just for her!

> "My heart is on fire, boiling over with passion. Bubbling up within me are these beautiful lyrics as a lovely poem to be sung for the King. Like a river bursting its banks, I'm overflowing with words, spilling out into this sacred story." Psalm 45:1 (TPT)

I highly recommend this masterpiece for anyone who desires to hear the sweet voice of the Lover of their soul, Jesus Christ.

Carol Krum
Healing Rooms Ministries

Sharon Swain is not only a dear friend; she is an anointed writer. Her books are not just "poetry;" they are a life spent intimately at the feet of Jesus. Each page you read reflects her journey with her Savior. Her writings are from the very heart of The Father, beckoning you to join them on this journey and to draw deep from the Living Words

inspired by the heart of The Father written on the pages within. What a blessing we've been given to also come and sit with Him face to face. I know you will be as blessed in the journey as I have been.

Naomi Krstinic
Crosses of Hope Ministry

Time flew by, and I felt such peace while reading Sharon's anointed poetry. Her writing draws you in and places your focus on the Lord and on who you are in Him very quickly. The world we live in carries many burdens and distractions. "Walking in Favor—Stepping into Grace" will take you away from those burdens and distractions as you read words sent from above.

Debbie Andrews Smith
Author, Echoes of His Heart

Favor?! Grace?! Who doesn't want more of these in our lives?! Through her moments with God, Sharon lets us see how to depend on God's favor and grace in the actual ups and downs of life. Her poetry captures the essence of growing in intimacy with our God who loves us so dearly. Expect to grow more in love with Him as you learn how to walk in favor and step into grace.

Sharon Hyatt
Long-Time Friend, Intercessor, and Beloved Daughter of God

Sharon's poetry is our beautiful invitation to daily "Come to Him" in all our moments. Through her voice, we hear the Shepherd's Voice—loving us, drawing us, and persuading us to come away with Him to a quiet place and rest awhile in His Love. You are in store for a precious gift of refreshment, rest, and hope.

Debi Finklea
Counselor, Operation 220 Ministries

I have had the privilege and honor of experiencing God's Word with Sharon for the last ten years in Bible study. Listening to and dwelling on her poems as they emerged has been a privilege, as has watching her growth and development towards this new book. Each poem will bring you closer to God's grace and wonder!

Betty McBride
OT North Texas Therapy Innovations

"The words that Sharon pens will leave you encouraged and uplifted. You will encounter genuine grace and love and the call and embrace of a God who delights in you. Whenever I read Sharon's poetry, I feel I have read words spoken by God Himself. You will encounter grace and hope. You will encounter the vastly deep love of a God who desires a close relationship with each and every one of us."

Kim Rees
Wife, Mum, and Lover of God

FOREWORD

By Frank Friedmann, Our Resolute Hope

In our search to find and experience God, there are only two roads available for us to travel. One is the road of religious good works, the road of legalism, the road of performing for acceptance. This road cannot produce life because the subject of this road is our selves.

The other road is the road of faith, the road of grace, the road of receiving from God. This is the road that leads to life because the subject of this road is the Author and Perfecter of salvation, the Lord Jesus Christ.

Once we have made the choice to walk the road of faith in Jesus, we must ever keep Him the subject of our journey. On one side of this road is a cliff, a corruption of grace called license, where we use grace to justify our self-oriented pursuits in life instead of living the Christ-life of love.

On the other side of the road is another cliff, a corruption of grace called passivity, where, in the name of grace, we fail to walk in the exercise of faith, just as we received Him (Colossians 2:6).

But even when we remain on this road of grace, there is yet another danger, where we become enamored and consumed with the revelation instead of the Revealer. The revelation of the New Covenant is glorious. We have been made new, made right, identified as saints, forgiven of all, redeemed, restored...These are our possessions, but they are only our possession because the Person, the Lord Jesus, has made it so.

My dear friends, remember the words of Paul to the Philippians - he told them that this "one thing" was not to know the message or the doctrine, but to "know Him" (Philippians 3). Jesus is the way. He is the Truth. He is the life...It is in Him, that we live and move and have our very being. This is the glory, that we can know and experience Him...Who is our life (Colossians 3:3–4).

INTRODUCTION

I just "love" a well-planned vacation with family or friends, don't you? I went with my family this summer on a trip to France and the UK via planes, trains, cars, and taxicabs, but I was most personally involved in a LOT of walking... and I mean a LOT!! It was a time of great fun for all of us, though, and the best part about the trip was being with the ones I love so dearly!

At the time of publishing this book, I have been walking with Jesus for 46 years. I accepted Christ when I was 29 years old, so you can do the math. You guessed it; I am no spring chicken!

Yet, over the years I felt like I was "stuck" in my walk (thanks to the lies from the enemy) that brought pain from guilt, shame, regret, condemnation, and fear, to name a few. It seemed impossible for me to pull myself out. Maybe you have a list of lies that you're dealing with right now. Maybe you're feeling "stuck" as well.

But Jesus reached out His hand to me and lifted me out of my despair. He began to show me who I really was in Christ. He has given me His very own righteousness, so I am enough. I am in Him. (2 Corinthians 5:21). I am at rest in His love today because I know I am in union with Him. You are as well if you have accepted Christ into your life. If you have not made that decision yet, Jesus is reaching His hand out to you, my friend.

Come and walk with me on this journey through poetry. And these poems are written in first and third person because we are in a relationship with Him. (John 17:20–21). You are His poetry; did you know that?

"We have become his poetry, a re-created people that will fulfill the destiny He has given each of us, for we are

joined to Jesus, the Anointed One. Even before we were born, God planned in advance our destiny and the good works we would do to fulfill it!" Ephesians 2:10 (TPT)

Two very important words are woven throughout Scripture: FAVOR and GRACE. We will be, "Walking in Favor" and "Stepping into Grace." We will explore these words and discover they are the "stepping stones" in our walk with Jesus.

I have been given a gift to write poetry to brag on Jesus and His finished work on the cross. In my own personal journey, I have walked through almost every poem He has placed on my heart to pen for Him. What an amazing journey He has had me on, and I know the journey will continue. I pray you, too, are blessed by this poetry and each accompanying Scripture!

Our journeys are all so personal—so different! We are each His masterpiece, fitted for His glory. Jesus is not just going to be helping you on this journey, He will be your very Life, your union with Him, and your oneness. God with us – Immanuel (Matthew 1:23)!

Pack your bags. We'll be going through some rough terrain, up hills and down in valleys. We'll rest. We'll overlook mountaintops, but we'll be mostly walking. We'll be blazing some new trails and discovering new pathways together. Our tour guide will be Jesus! Now, He's not going to be just helping us as we blaze through this new trail, but He will live inside us and promises to never leave us or forsake us (Hebrews 13:5). Plus, He promises to go before us as well, so come listen for the Savior's voice and His "love call" to you. He will be speaking to you personally, my friend, out of His deep love for you. Are you ready?

Sharon Swain

YOUR JOURNEY IN JESUS

Now that you've chosen to pack your bags and have made the decision to join us on this journey, let's go, my friend! You are going to embark on a journey like no other you have ever been on before. Because Jesus now lives inside you, He won't just be beside you, helping you. He is now your Life!

- Jesus ultimately went before us in all things. His walk to the cross made our walk possible:

> "Therefore when Jesus had received the sour wine, He said, "It is finished!" John 19:30 (NASB20)

> "Now to Him who is able to do far more abundantly beyond all that we ask or think, according to the power that works within us." Ephesians 3:20 (NASB20)

- You will be listening to the voice of Jesus within. You will learn to hear His voice as you spend time in the Word of God:

> "My sheep hear My voice, and I know them, and they follow Me." John 10:27 (NASB20)

> "All Scripture is inspired by God and profitable for teaching, for reproof, for correction, for training in righteousness; so that the man of God may be adequate, equipped for every good work." 2 Timothy 3:16-17 (ESV)

- Now that you are a believer in Jesus, He will teach you how to walk in Him:

> "Therefore as you have received Christ Jesus the Lord, so walk in Him, rooted and built up in him and established in the faith..." Colossians 2:6-7a (ESV)

- You will be setting your sights on the "Kingdom of God" that is within you; not the "kingdom of the world "that you see outwardly. These two kingdoms are polar opposites from each other:

    > "But seek first His kingdom and His righteousness, and all these things will be given to you as well." Matthew 6:33 (NIV)

    > "Do not love the world nor the things in the world. If anyone loves the world, the love of the Father is not in him. For all that is in the world, the lust of the flesh and the lust of the eyes and the boastful pride of life, is not from the Father, but is from the world." 1 John 2:15-16 (ESV)

- You will be walking by faith and not by sight:

    > "Therefore, being always of good courage, and knowing that while we are at home in the body we are absent from the Lord—for we walk by faith, not by sight..." 2 Corinthians 5:6-7 (NASB20)

- You will get to know Him on this journey of life, not just when you get to heaven:

  "...that I may know Him and
  the power of His resurrection
  and fellowship of His sufferings,
  being conformed to His death;
  if somehow I may attain to the
  resurrection from the dead."
  Philippians 3:10-11 (NASB20)

- Joy and peace will be yours when you walk in the Spirit and not the flesh:

  "But the fruit of the Spirit
  is love, joy, peace, patience,
  kindness, goodness, faithfulness,
  gentleness, self-control; against
  such things there is no law."
  Galatians 5:22-23 (ESV)

- When Jesus died on the cross, He established a brand-New Covenant for us to walk in:

  "But now He has obtained
  a more excellent ministry,
  to the extent that He is also
  the mediator of a better
  covenant, which has been
  enacted on better promises."
  Hebrews 8:6 (NASB20)

> "This is the covenant I will make with the people of Israel after that time," declares the LORD. "I will put my law in their minds and write it on their hearts. I will be their God, and they will be my people." Jeremiah 31:33 (NIV)

- You have been given new wants and desires:

> "Therefore if anyone is in Christ, he is a new creature. The old has passed away; behold, the new has come." 2 Corinthians 5:17 (ESV)

> "Moreover, I will give you a new heart and put a new spirit within you; and I will remove the heart of stone from your flesh and give you a heart of flesh." Ezekiel 36:26 (NASB20)

- You are enough because you are now in Him. Rest in His finished work on the cross. Let this verse sink deeply in your heart! You have been given His very own righteousness:

> "For God made the only one who did not know sin to become sin for us, so that we might become the righteousness of God through our union with Him." 2 Corinthians 5:21 (TPT)

Ultimately, our final journey one day will be to live with Him for all eternity, but for now, enjoy the journey with Him in the here and now. His love, favor, and grace will "whisper on your heart" and lead the way!

"WALKING IN FAVOR"

"Favor is what opens up doors no man can shut, favor is what puts you in places you know you don't have no business being in. Favor is what sets you in positions that you know you weren't qualified for. Favor is what makes it so that you are exactly where you're supposed to be to accomplish exactly what it is that God has set for you to accomplish. It's what qualifies you when you don't have the degree and you don't have the diploma. You don't have the connections. You're just where God has opened up a door for you to be. Even though people might talk badly about you or try to push you out of that place, you cannot be moved. Not because you manufactured your way there, but because God's Spirit has placed you there. God's Spirit on your life is what makes it so that you don't have to market yourself because you've already been marked by the presence of the Almighty God." - Priscilla Shirer[1]

---

1. Shirer, Priscilla. "Living Your Life for Christ." Speech. Propel Women's Conference, Fayetteville, AR. September 2, 2018. [35:39-36:24] Recorded. https://www.youtube.com/watch?v=yjtvD1dpXjw.

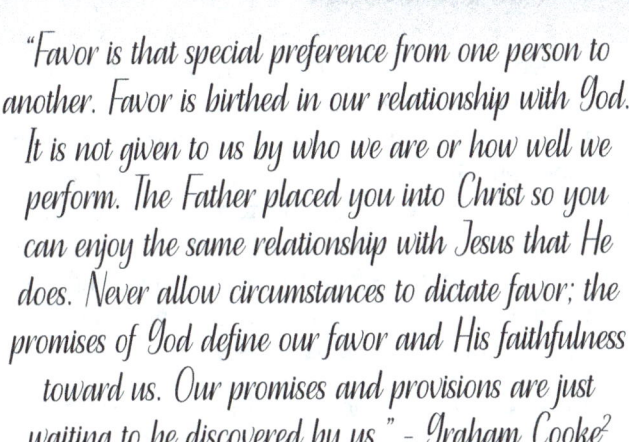

"Favor is that special preference from one person to another. Favor is birthed in our relationship with God. It is not given to us by who we are or how well we perform. The Father placed you into Christ so you can enjoy the same relationship with Jesus that He does. Never allow circumstances to dictate favor; the promises of God define our favor and His faithfulness toward us. Our promises and provisions are just waiting to be discovered by us." - Graham Cooke[2]

Favor comes from believing in Jesus Christ. We receive all the spiritual blessings in the heavenly realms from the Father because we are united with Christ. (Ephesians 1:3)

- Jesus found favor with God and with people. (Luke 2:52)
- Mary, the mother of Jesus, found favor with the Lord. (Luke 1:25, 30)
- The early church found favor with people and had the blessing of the Lord on them. (Acts 2:47)
- David found favor with the Lord. (Acts 7:46)
- Moses found favor in the sight of God. (Exodus 33:17)
- Ruth found favor with Boaz because of God's goodness. (Ruth 2:2, 10, 13)
- Samuel found favor with the Lord and with people (1 Samuel 2:26)
- Esther found favor and kindness with her king. (Esther 2:17)
- David found favor with the Lord. (Acts 7:46)

---

2. Cooke, Graham. "Favor is Birthed in Relationship." *Brilliant Perspectives*. 20 July, 2016. https://brilliantperspectives.com/favor-is-a-relationship/

"STEPPING INTO GRACE"

By Tim Chalas, Grace Life Fellowship

Grace does not lead to sin, give a license to sin, or excuse sin: it is the empowerment for righteousness. Grace never needs to be balanced or over-corrected. Grace is not opposed to works; it is opposed to merit by works. Grace is not a part of the gospel; it is the gospel. Grace does not mean God looks past your sin; it means He did something about it. Grace means you are not too far gone and that no matter what you have done, it's not too late. There is nothing you have done for which grace is not greater still. Grace means there's hope, what allows us to move forward instead of staying stuck. Grace means that right now, at this very moment, is a new beginning. Today is a new day, and tomorrow now has a new hope.

- Because of grace, David moved from a murderer to a man after God's own heart. (1 Samuel 13:14; Acts 13:22)
- Because of grace, Saul the persecutor became Paul the preacher. (1 Corinthians 15:9-10)
- Because of grace, Peter went from a denier to a declarer of Jesus. (Matthew 26:75; Acts 2:14-42)

If there's hope for the people in the Bible, and that's just a few examples, there's hope for us, too. Because of grace, you are never a lost cause, and you are never too far gone. There is no shelf-life with grace! Because of grace, what may haunt you is never greater than what heals you. Because of grace, we move from rules to relationship, from law to love. Because of grace, we move from fear to freedom. Because of grace, we move from trying to trusting. Grace is not just a doctrine, a belief system, or a lifestyle. Grace is certainly not just something we say before a meal; grace **is** the meal, whereby God meets our deepest hunger by placing His very life into us, to live His life through us. Grace is embodied in the person of Jesus Christ, who brings us into a dynamic relationship with the living God.

> "For the grace of God has appeared, bringing salvation for all people, training us to renounce ungodliness and worldly passions, and to live self-controlled, upright, and godly lives in the present age…" Titus 2:11-12 (ESV)

> "For the Law was given through Moses; grace and truth were realized through Jesus Christ." John 1:17 (NASB20)

> "And the Word became flesh, and dwelt among us; and we saw His glory, glory as of the only Son from the Father, full of grace and truth." John 1:14 (NASB20)

THE SAME GRACE THAT BRINGS YOU TO JESUS IS THE SAME GRACE THAT GROWS YOU IN JESUS.

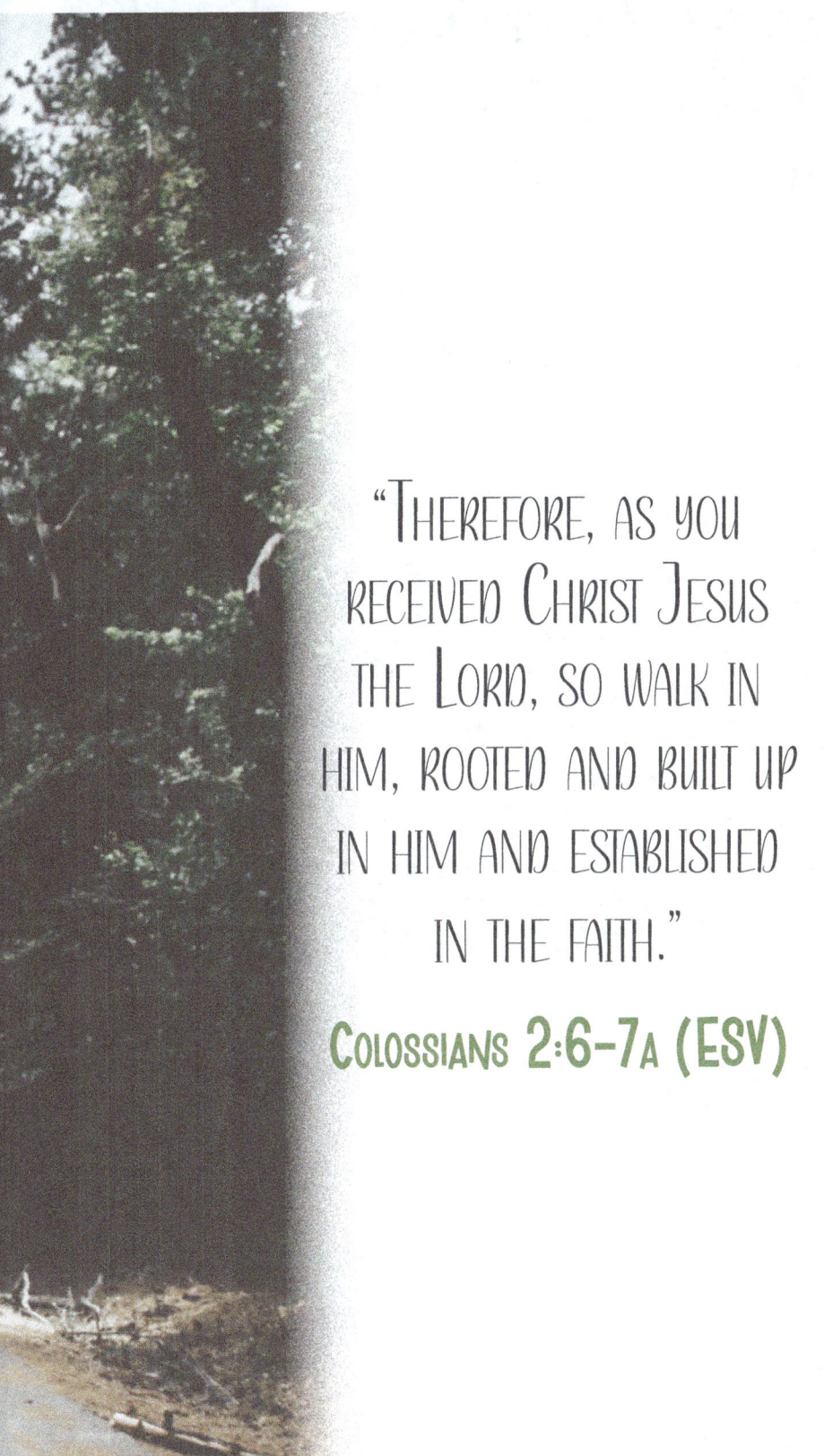

"Therefore, as you received Christ Jesus the Lord, so walk in him, rooted and built up in him and established in the faith."

Colossians 2:6-7a (ESV)

HIS
PEACE

"For to us a child is born, to us a son is given, and the government will be on his shoulders. And his name shall be called Wonderful Counselor, Mighty God, Everlasting Father, Prince of Peace."

Isaiah 9:6 (ESV)

There's always been great turmoil in the world, and that's obviously still the case today. However, because Jesus now lives in your heart, He has promised you Himself, who is your peace. As a believer, He gives you His supernatural peace. Certainly, all your problems don't always go away at the time you want them to, but He will calm your heart down in the midst of your struggles:

"Behold, He who keeps Israel will neither slumber nor sleep." Psalm 121:4 (ESV)

That means He does not need sleep, and you are always in His care. He does not even doze off like we would probably do. He stays awake all night guarding you and keeping you. He is God, and He is sovereign. Each and every event and situation is under God's sovereign rule and control.

His peace is internal because He lives in your heart now that you're a believer in Jesus. He promises to calm your troubled heart:

"Peace I leave you, My peace I give to you; not as the world gives, do I give to you. Do not let your hearts be troubled, nor fearful." John 14:27 (NASB20)

"Do not let your heart be troubled; believe in God, believe also in Me." John 14:1 (NASB20)

Jesus is your supernatural and internal peace that does not make sense to the outside world:

"The steadfast of mind You will keep in perfect peace, Because he trusts in You." Isaiah 26:3 (NASB20)

"Now may the Lord of peace Himself continually grant you peace in every circumstance. The Lord be with you all!" 2 Thessalonians 3:16 (NASB 20)

When walking through the storms of life, He is your Peace!

YOU'RE SECURE IN HIS LOVE!

A BRAND NEW DAY

This day is shining brightly;
It's different than the past.
It's bringing rays of
Hope and change—
A brand new day at last!

A brand new day in You
'Cause the new is what You do.
A mighty rushing wind
In the "secret place" with Him.

"Come up here with Me"
Is His whisper to my heart.
There's freshness in the air
With a message to impart.

Come linger in My love
And take some time to hear.
Just sit alone with Me;
Let Me take your doubts and fears.

There's no time for past regrets
So take My hand and will you let
Me speak new hope and change
And let's make the big exchange.

Stop trying on your own.
We're now one; you're not alone.
My life was placed in you
And My love will see you through.

I am your hope of glory
And I have your plans and story.
I'll fashion out your day
Because I am the Way!

I am the One who rescued you.
You're not the same; you were made new.
Right from the day you first believed,
For I'm in you and you're in Me!

"... Christ in you, the hope of glory." Colossians 1:27 (ESV)

"The glory which You have given Me I also have given to them, so that they may be one, just as We are one; I in them and You in Me, that they may be perfected in unity, so that the world may know that You sent Me, and You loved them, just as You loved Me." John 17:22-23 (NASB 20)

A NEW LENS

A new path, a new way
Was carved out for you.
He didn't patch up the old
But made you brand new!

He's not holding your hand
And walking beside,
But made you His home
And now lives inside.

Christ is in you
And you are in Him.
He gave you Himself
To peer from a new lens.

An exchange did take place
And your sins He erased.
The old you was replaced
With Himself to embrace.

He doesn't show up
Just to depart,
But made you His home
And now lives in your heart.

You're righteous in Him
For His death took your sin
And you now have His power
To walk in this hour.

So touch up your thinking
And believe you're brand new.
You'll see out of a new lens
With new focus in view!

REFLECTIONS AFTER A TEACHING BY
GRAHAM COOKE, BRILLIANT PERSPECTIVES

"Or do you not know that all of us who have been baptized into Christ Jesus have been baptized into His death? Therefore we have been buried with Him through baptism into death, so that, just as Christ was raised from the dead through the glory of the Father, so we too may walk in newness of life. For if we have become united with Him in the likeness of His death, certainly we shall also be in the likeness of His resurrection." Romans 6:3-5 (NASB20)

"Therefore, if anyone is in Christ, he is a new creation. The old things passed away; behold, the new has come." 2 Corinthians 5:17 (ESV)

"He made Him who knew no sin to be sin in our behalf, so that we might become the righteousness of God in Him." 2 Corinthians 5:21 (NASB20)

A TIME TO MOURN

A time to mourn,
He knows your loss.
You've suffered much
At quite a cost.

You have the Christ
That lives in you.
He knows your needs;
He'll see you through,
For it's His job to care for you.

This unsure path
You're walking down;
He'll lead and guide
Without a sound.

He'll make things clear;
He'll dry your tears.
He'll give you peace;
He'll calm your fears.

He'll be your rest
For He knows best.
You'll sense His love
Deep in your chest.

A time to mourn,
He knows your pain.
You've suffered much;
He knows your name.

"A time to weep and a time to laugh; A time to mourn and a time to dance." Ecclesiastes 3:4 (NASB20)

"Blessed are those who mourn, for they shall be comforted." Matthew 5:4 (ESV)

ALL MY TOMORROWS

My tomorrows are not here
But they beckon afar.
They stir up my fears
That are far out of reach
Just like distant stars.

So to You do I cling
And my tomorrows I bring.
I hand over that thing
That worries me so.

My journey I give
Because I am Yours,
And when my thoughts
Are in turmoil,
You calm my roars.

So help me to trust
And gently let go
And believe You know best
Because You said so.

'Cause all my tomorrows,
And even my sorrows,
Are wrapped in Your love
Straight from above.

No need then to borrow
Or grab hold of tomorrow
'Cause each one of my days
Is numbered by You.

They'll show up on the scene
In the order ordained,
And my tomorrows will bring
Your love with the dew.

"So do not worry about tomorrow; for tomorrow will worry about itself. Each day has enough trouble of its own." Matthew 6:34 (NASB20)

AN INNER INVITATION

Come go with me, My child.
There's so much more to see,
For I will lead and guide within
So come and follow Me.

You're wandering in the desert
And feeling all alone,
But I died upon that cross for you
So your heart could be My home.

I will whisper oh so gently;
I'll be your comfort zone.
My Life now lives inside of you
And My love will lead you home.

Together we will face each day
For I am the Great, "I Am!"
You'll no longer sense you're all alone;
Step out and trust My plan.

Your sins were all forgiven
At the cross so long ago.
You asked Me in; I forgave your sins.
Now you're flawless; don't you know?

My love will be your story,
For you're chosen for My glory.
We'll walk together, you and Me,
And I'll remind you that you're free.

You are complete in Me
And wrapped in royalty,
And the power of My Presence
Will free you to believe.

I'm your resurrection power
For each and every hour.
We'll fellowship;
We're one, you know.
So walk with Me;
Let's go!

"It was for freedom that Christ set us free; therefore keep standing firm and do not be subject again to a yoke of slavery." Galatians 5:1 (NASB20)

"The glory which You have given Me I also have given to them, so that they may be one, just as We are one, I in them and You in Me, that they may be perfected in unity, so that the world may know that You sent Me, and You loved them, just as You loved Me." John 17:22-23 (NASB20)

AN ORIGINAL

An original,
That's who you are.
God broke the mold.
You are His heart.

You've been in His plan
Since time began.
Uniquely formed
By the Great, "I Am."

In His image
He created you.
A duplicate
Would never do.

A masterpiece
Bought with a price.
God sent His Son,
Your sacrifice.

He bought you back
With His own Life.
The highest price
So do not strive.

Don't look around
Do not compare.
He has your plans,
Though unaware.

With purpose clear
The day, the year.
They will unfold
From days of old.

Give Him your yes
Who loves you best.
His masterpiece—
So trust and rest!

"So God created man in his own image, in the image of God He created him; male and female he created them." Genesis 1:27 (ESV)

"For God so loved the world, that he gave his one and only Son, that whoever believes in him should not perish but have eternal life." John 3:16 (NIV)

BRIDGING THE GAP

Your thundering voice
Is rumbling outside,
Yet I sit here with You,
And You live inside.

Your Majesty reigns
Over all of the earth,
Yet You whisper to me
Of my value and worth.

You open the heavens
And loudly declare,
Yet You speak to my heart
And tell me You care.

Volcanoes erupting
And earthquakes abound,
Yet I hear Your voice
With no rumble or sound.

You open the heavens
And declare Your great Name,
Yet You've taken my guilt
And removed all my shame.

Oh, the expanse of the oceans,
Valleys and seas,
Yet You bridged the gap
And brought Jesus to me.

"The heavens declare the glory of God, and the sky above proclaims his handiwork." Psalm 19:1 (ESV)

"...Christ in you, the hope of glory."
Colossians 1:27b (NASB20)

COME TO JESUS

Come to Jesus
A simple plea
He died for you
Upon that tree.

Come to Jesus
Confess your sin
Believe He died
And rose again.

Come to Jesus
Be born again
You'll know His love
He'll call you friend.

Come to Jesus
He's coming soon
Maybe morning
Maybe noon.

Come to Jesus
His love is true
He knows your name
He's calling you.

Come to Jesus
Give Him your yes
You'll know His love
His peace and rest.

"...for all have sinned and fall short of the glory of God." Romans 3:23 (NIV)

"that if you confess with your mouth Jesus as Lord, and believe in your heart that God raised Him from the dead, you will be saved; for with the heart a person believes, resulting in righteousness, and with the mouth he confesses, resulting in salvation." Romans 10:9-10 (NASB20)

"Jesus answered him, 'Truly, truly, I say to you, unless one is born again he cannot see the kingdom of God.'" John 3:3 (ESV)

EMPTY SPACES

In your darkest space,
There's a Savior filled with grace,
Who chose to take your sin,
Who will love you to the end.

He'll be your hiding place,
And He never will forsake;
Nor will you want to run
When you're captured by the Son.

He knows your deepest needs
And, in Him, He will exceed
All your heart's desires when
His flame sets you on fire!

He'll be your closest friend
And, In Him, He will defend,
And heal your deepest sorrows,
Who holds all your tomorrows.

So let Him fill your space
And receive His gift of grace,
Who died to make you new
And will fill that void in you.

He'll drive the dark away
With Himself, who is the Way,
And you will be made new
With His love, replaced in you!

"That if you confess with your mouth Jesus as Lord, and believe in your heart that God raised Him from the dead, you will be saved; for with the heart a person believes, resulting in righteousness, and with the mouth he confesses, resulting in salvation." Romans 10:9-10 (NASB20)

"You are my hiding place; You keep me from trouble; You surround me with songs of deliverance." Psalm 32:7 (NASB20)

EVEN THOUGH

Even though
The days drag on,
He is my joy—
He is my song.

Even though
The valley's deep,
He gives me hope—
He is my peace.

Even though
Death looms so near,
He takes my hand
And calms my fears.

Even though
The table's set,
The enemy's plans—
My God upsets.

Even though
Evil's all about,
My victory's sure—
I'll shout it out!

Even though
I question why,
Jesus lives in me—
I won't deny.

Even though
Fears do abound,
His peace leaves me—
Now settled down.

"Do not be anxious about anything, but in every situation, by prayer and petition, with thanksgiving, present your requests to God. And the peace of God, which transcends all understanding, will guard your hearts and your minds in Christ Jesus." Philippians 4:6-7 (NIV)

"Peace I leave with you; my peace I give to you. Not as the world gives do I give to you. Let not your hearts be troubled, neither let them be afraid." John 14:27 (ESV)

HE'LL LEAD YOU HOME

Winds and waves
Toss to and fro;
Back and forth;
The storms do blow.

Tossed about,
Those storms of life.
Fears and doubts
And lots of strife.

But don't lose hope;
He's in your boat.
Christ lives in you;
He's your rescue.

He is your help,
But more than that,
He's now your Life;
That is a fact.

He'll be to you
Just what you need.
Just trust His heart
And do believe.

He's got the oars;
He'll lead you home,
So let Him lead;
You're not alone.

He is your Guide;
Your GPS.
He is the Way;
Your happiness.

The Christ in you
Is all you need.
He died for you
To set you free!

"...to whom God willed to make known what is the wealth of the glory of this mystery among the Gentiles is, the mystery that is Christ in you, the hope of glory."' Colossians 1:27 (NASB20)

"When He got into the boat, His disciples followed Him." Matthew 8:23 (NASB20)

"It was for freedom that Christ set us free..." Galatians 5:1a (NASB20)

HIDE ME AWAY

Hide me away
From the cares of the day
Away from the world
And all its charade.

Let me just drink
From Your deep well above
And sit with You, Jesus,
And be held in Your love.

High up above
In the cleft of the Rock
So secluded above
Where we can just talk.

Hide me away
Oh, a time just for us
Away from the hustle,
The noise and the fuss.

Let me just bask
And lean into You
While the world is astir
And always in view.

To be found in Your love
And desire You first;
To drink from Your well
And be quenched of my thirst.

Oh, hide me away
From the cares of the day
As I wait for Your whisper
While I read and I pray.

"For in the day of trouble he will keep me safe in his dwelling; he will hide me in the shelter of his sacred tent and set me high upon a rock." Psalm 27:5 (NIV)

"Your word is a lamp to guide my feet and a light for my path." Psalm 119:105 (NLT)

"...let anyone who is thirsty come to me and drink. Whoever believes in me, as Scripture has said, rivers of living water will flow from within them." John 7:37-38 (NIV)

I'VE CHOSEN YOU

The storms have come
The storms have gone
But you, my child,
Have just hung on.

You've clung to Me
Right by My side
You are My joy;
My deep delight.

You've listened well
You've heard my voice
You've borne much fruit
It was your choice.

The days are new
I've chosen you
New heights we'll reach
Just Me and you!

So climb with Me
And don't look down.
New fruit we'll pick
Where love abounds.

Just hold on tight
We're climbing high
Where air is thin
Up in the sky.

"Listen! My beloved! Behold, he is coming, leaping on the mountains, jumping on the hills!" Song of Solomon 2:8 (NASB20)

"And many peoples will come and say, 'Come, let's go up to the mountain of the Lord, To the house of the God of Jacob; So that He may teach us about His ways, And that we may walk in His paths.' For the law will go out from Zion And the word of the Lord from Jerusalem." Isaiah 2:3 (NASB20)

IMAGINARY CAGES

You are complete in Christ
And did you know you've been set free?
No longer are you bound up tight
But you now have liberty!

Regret and condemnation,
Guilt, defeat, and shame
Have had you living in the past,
Along with fear and blame.

Believing lies you thought were true
Have caused distress and doubt,
But did you know, oh precious child,
Jesus came to sort things out.

The enemy has locked you up
And thinks he has the key,
But you, dear one,
Have been made new;
For you are free indeed!

Those imaginary cages
Built up within your mind;
He'll tear them down.
Give them to Him,
And leave them all behind.

He gave His Life
To set you free;
To heal your hurts and more.
He is the Way, the Truth,
The Life,
And all you're longing for!

"It is for freedom that Christ has set us free. Stand firm, then, and do not let yourselves be burdened again by a yoke of slavery." Galatians 5:1 (NIV)

"For though we walk in the flesh, we do not wage battle according to the flesh, for the weapons of our warfare are not of the flesh, but divinely powerful for the destruction of fortresses. We are destroying arguments and all arrogance raised against the knowledge of God, and we are taking every thought captive to the obedience of Christ..." 2 Corinthians 10:3-5

IT'S TIME

It's time to just let go
And let Me rearrange;
It's time to look My way
And take the big exchange.

It's time to find new joy in Me
And hear My voice within.
I'm waiting here to say so much
Because you are My friend.

You're part of My big plan;
You've been crucified with Me
And no longer are you all alone;
It's about just you and Me!

So trust Me, child.
I am Your Life,
So walk by faith with Me.
Stop trying to control
Your life;
Just look to Me,
Believe!

In the midst of life's demands,
Your life is in My hands.
You were made new,
Your heart was changed;
I am your biggest fan.

The exchange was made;
I paid the price.
I died to set you free
So you'd know life
Eternal life,
And find that Life in Me!

"I have been crucified with Christ. It is no longer I who live, but Christ who lives in me. And the life I now live in the flesh I live by faith in the Son of God, who loved me and gave himself for me." Galatians 2:20 (ESV)

LIFT YOUR LOAD

In the quiet of the moment
As I lean against Your chest,
I hear You whisper gently;
Come sit with Me and rest.

Your troubles, they are mounting
And they've got you weighted down.
It shows for sure in all you do
'Cause you wear that frown around.

So drop that load; give it to Me;
It's too heavy for your back.
I'll lift your load and give you peace;
I'll take those worries from your sack.

That's why We're one; just you and Me.
No need to waste your day
Because, my child, My precious child,
You're to give My love away.

Oh, they won't see Me working, dear,
If you're fretting all day long
So drop that load, give it to Me,
Let's sing a brand new song.

Just rest awhile; put on a smile,
I'll supply the joy within.
Just yield to Me; give Me your load
And look to Me, my friend!

"Come to Me, all who are weary and burdened, and I will give you rest. Take my yoke upon you and learn from me, for I am gentle and humble in heart, and you will find rest for your souls. For my yoke is easy and my burden is light." Matthew 11:28-30 (NIV)

MY CALLED-OUT ONE

Set apart;
My called-out one.
I've chosen you;
We've just begun.

So listen up:
I'll fill your cup.
Lean into to Me,
For we are One.

You listen well.
You hear My voice.
You are the one;
You are My choice.

Your fingerprints
They match the time.
I'll use you, child;
You were designed.

To walk with Me,
Hear from the heart.
You know My will;
My words impart.

Don't be afraid;
Don't run and hide.
My arms outstretched,
They're open wide.

Your fingerprints;
They are unique.
They match the call
Of your gifted speech.

So just step forth
And walk with Me!
I proved My love;
I set you free.

I paved the way
To eternity
When I walked
That road to Calvary.

> "You whom I have taken from the ends of the earth and called from its remotest parts, and said to you, 'You are My servant, I have chosen you and have not rejected you.'" Isaiah 41:9 (NASB20)

> "They took Jesus, therefore, and He went out, carrying His own cross, to the place called the Place of a Skull, which in Hebrew is called, Golgotha. There they crucified Him, and with Him two other men, one on either side, and Jesus in between." John 19:17-18 (NASB20)

NEW LIFE IN HIM

Life is found in Him alone.
He knows your name;
You're not alone.

He's searching, child,
Throughout the earth.
He's calling you;
Your prayers are heard.

He'll give you Life,
A second birth.
He knows your pain;
He knows your worth.

He looked through time
And saw your face.
He died for you
To take your place.

This is the hour
He's calling you.
Just say yes
To His embrace.

Give Him your yes
Above the rest.
You're #1,
Not second best.

The Master holds
New Life in Him.
Receive Him now.
He calls you friend!

"...that if you confess with your mouth Jesus as Lord, and believe in your heart that God raised Him from the dead, you will be saved; for with the heart a person believes, resulting in righteousness, and with the mouth he confesses, resulting in salvation." Romans 10:9-10 (NASB20)

ONCE AND FOR ALL

No need to dwell
Upon the past.
You're new in Christ;
You're free at last!

You're righteous, child.
Jesus paid the price.
He took your sin;
He sacrificed.

You're blameless now
Once and for all,
His blood applied,
So stand up tall!

You're one with Him;
He paid your debt.
Don't drag around
Guilt or regret.

Once for all time,
No need for more.
His blood was shed.
Your sins He bore.

So remember Him
And not your sin.
His love wins out
Without a doubt.

Paid in full
It's finished now.
Your sins are gone,
So don't allow

Doubt or defeat;
You are complete,
So don't let Satan
Grab your seat.

You're in heavenly places;
You're seated now.
You're no longer lost,
But now you're found!

"He did not enter by means of the blood of goats and calves; but he entered the Most Holy Place once for all by his own blood, thus obtaining eternal redemption." Hebrews 9:12 (NIV)

"But God, being rich in mercy, because of His great love with which He loved us, even when we were dead in our wrongdoings, made us alive together with Christ, (by grace you have been saved), and raised us up with Him, and seated us with Him in the heavenly places in Christ Jesus, so that in the ages to come He might show the boundless riches of His grace in kindness towards us in Christ Jesus." Ephesians 2:4-7 (NASB20)

OPEN DOOR POLICY

Come boldly, child.
I'm waiting here.
My throne is grace.
Come gently peer

Into My heart
For you today.
Come linger, child.
Come sit and stay

For just a while.
Come bring your needs
And lay them out.
Just talk to Me.

You're welcome here.
Come boldly bring
What troubles you—
That gnawing thing
That's in your view.

You're righteous, child.
I made you new.
Bask in My love;
I died for you.

The veil was rent
And ripped in two.
My blood poured out
So I'd know you.

I made a way
So you could say
What troubles you;
I am the Way,

The Truth, the Life.
I know your plight.
Just talk to Me.
I'll shed new light.

Come boldly, child.
You're weighted down.
I'll lift your load;
I wore your crown.

> "Let us then approach God's throne of grace with confidence, so that we may receive mercy and find grace to help us in our time of need." Hebrews 4:16 (NIV)

REST IN ME

Stop striving, child of Mine.
Come sit with Me and dine
Upon My Word today,
And peace I'll send your way.

Let go of all your cares,
For there's trouble everywhere.
But I'm the God who sees
And can handle all your needs.

I've loved you from the start,
And I see your troubled heart.
So sit with Me awhile
And focus now, my child.

It's time to rest in Me,
So trust and just believe
That I know all your needs
And will guide you faithfully.

I'll calm you down inside,
So rest and just abide.
Come listen for My voice
As you pull away by choice.

And when you pull away
And give Me time today,
You'll discover all along
That in Me you do belong.

Then when you do get up,
You'll know I've filled your cup.
For you've rested in My love,
Sent down from up above.

My peace you'll surely know
In My rest before you go.
For Life is found in Me
And in Me you are complete!

"Come to Me, all who are weary and burdened, and I will give you rest. Take my yoke upon you and learn from me, for I am gentle and humble in heart, and you will find rest for your souls. For my yoke is easy and my burden is light." Matthew 11:28-30 (NIV)

SITTING WITH THE MASTER

Sitting with the Master,
Oh, the union that we share.
The love inside my heart
Lets me know that He is there.

Pulling close to Jesus
And basking in His love
Brings comfort and assurance
'Cause I know He is enough.

He calms me down
And brings assurance through His Word.
He satisfies my longings,
And my prayers
Are always heard.

Sitting with the Master
Brings the glue to solve my day.
Just to know He lives inside my heart
Helps me know I'll be ok.

His grace so freely given
Has found a home in me
'Cause sitting with the Master
Gives me peace and liberty!

"Early in the morning He came again to the temple. All the people came to him, and he sat down and taught them." John 8:2 (ESV)

"...fixing our eyes on Jesus, the pioneer and perfecter of faith. For the joy set before him he endured the cross, scorning its shame, and sat down at the right hand of the throne of God." Hebrews 12:2 (NIV)

THAT STILL, SMALL VOICE

Listen closely
For My voice.
Lean in, My child,
Above the noise.

Expectant voices
All around
Are not of Me
And drag you down.

Caught in a web
And tied in knots
As you're left wrestling
With your thoughts.

Jagged edges,
Raw and bleeding
From others pleading
To fit their mold
From what you're told.

But your plans
Are in My hands.
Watch them unfold;
I'm the great, "I Am!"

My voice is gentle,
Kind and tender.
Learn to discern
And stay alert.

I sacrificed
To make it right.
I died for you;
I paid the price.

My Word is key,
So learn of Me.
I will not hide
But lead and guide.

So give Me time
And do not quit.
My love will mold
Your perfect fit.

Just hear My voice
Above the roar,
For I'm the One
You're searching for!

> "And after the fire came a gentle whisper." 1 Kings 19:12 (NIV)

> "My sheep listen to My voice, and I know them, and they follow Me..." John 10:27 (NASB20)

THAT STONY HEART

The stone was rolled away that day
To give me hope anew;
To replace that stony heart of mine
And make it all brand new;
To take that emptiness away
And fill it up with You.

For I had death and needed life;
So the struggle did ensue,
But God had a plan to rescue man
And make us all brand new.

And then one day, out of the blue,
Good news, it reached my ear
That Jesus died to take MY sin
And free me from MY fears.

So on that day, so long ago,
He pulled me close to Him.
He took my sin and entered in,
And I was born again.

And so, you, too, can find new Life
Just like I did that day,
For I was lost and far away,
And now He's here to stay.

He'll roll that stone away for you
And give you Life within.
He'll take your sin;
He'll be your friend,
And new Life will then begin.

No longer will there be a void
'Cause He'll fill your heart with love,
And new Life He'll give to you, my friend,
Sent down from heaven above.

"Moreover, I will give you a new heart and put a new spirit within you; and I will remove the heart of stone from your flesh and give you a heart of flesh." Ezekiel 36:26 (NASB20)

"Very early on the first day of the week, just after sunrise, they were on their way to the tomb, and they asked each other, 'Who will roll the stone away from the entrance of the tomb?' But when they looked up, they saw that the stone, which was very large, had been rolled away." Mark 16:2-4 (NIV)

UNION STATION

You've pulled out of the station,
But don't be mistaken,
For on this new path you've found
And have recently taken,
You'll never, no never,
Again be forsaken.

For this union you've chosen
Can never be broken.
You were sealed with His Spirit
Because you were chosen.

You've been given new power
From the head of the Tower.
For His Spirit lives in you,
And a new path is in view.

So lean into Him
And know He's your friend,
For He lives within
And has taken your sin.

You're now heaven-bound;
You're not lost, but you're found.
You've found Union Station
And can never be shaken.

So be blessed and just rest
And lean into His chest.
You're now powered with love
Straight from above.

For you've found salvation
At Union Station,
So choose by His Spirit
To walk in His ways.

And you'll know
Brand new freedom
At Union Station,
Empowered by Him
For all of your days!

"For if we have become united with Him in the likeness of His death, certainly we shall also be in the likeness of His resurrection..." Romans 6:5 (NASB20)

"But if you live in life-union with me and if my words live powerfully within you—then you can ask whatever you desire and it will be done." John 15:7 (TPT)

"....even more of God's comfort will cascade upon us through our union with Christ." 2 Corinthians 1:5 (TPT)

VALLEYS BELOW

There's myrrh in the valley
And freshness below;
There's a look at the Savior
With His love all aglow.

For this valley is deep
And laden with thorns,
But I'm hidden in Christ,
And together we weather
The depths of the storm.

There's suffering involved,
But He's calling my name.
This valley is deep
With no fortune or fame.

Oh, a glimpse of
The pain and suffering for me
As He hung and He suffered
For my sin on that tree.

But a look at the Savior
As I glance in His eyes
Brings a new sense of trust
As His love is my guide.

So we walk down this path
As I cling to His side,
And I now walk in Him
Because I am His bride.

Now He's rearranged me,
And new hope is alive
As I walk with the Savior,
Share in His death,
And know He's my Life!

"...that I may know him and the power of his resurrection, and may share his sufferings, becoming like him in his death..." Philippians 3:10 (ESV)

"Until the cool of the day when the shadows flee, I will go my way to the mountain of myrrh and to the hill of frankincense." Song of Solomon 4:6 (NASB20)

WALKIN' AND ALL WOBBLY

I'm walkin' and all wobbly,
And I don't get it right,
But His love keeps me walkin'
So I know I'm all right.

Just like a child
Who wobbles and falls down,
His arms are outstretched
As I fall to the ground.

But He picks me up
And tells me to trust,
To look straight at Him,
For He's made quite a fuss.

He walked to the cross
And died in my place.
He took all my sins,
And now they're erased.

Oh, I will walk wobbly,
And still I'll fall down,
But His love lifts me up
When I fall to the ground.

He's the Light of the World,
And He lives in my heart.
I am complete in His love,
And He never departs.

Oh, sometimes I'm wobbly
When I step out in sin,
But His love draws me back
'Cause Jesus lives in.

I'm still a mess,
But my heart was made new.
I'm righteous in Him,
So He'll see me through.

Oh, I've got a friend
Who knows about you;
He's your "fixer upper,"
And He died for you, too!

> "My sheep listen to My voice, and I know them, and they follow Me..." John 10:27 (NASB20)

> "Therefore, as you received Christ Jesus the Lord, so walk in him, rooted and built up in him and established in the faith..." Colossians 2:6-7a (ESV)

WALKING IN THE VALLEY

Walking hand in hand with You,
The treacherous terrain's in view.
A narrow path, a downward slope,
I'm weary, Lord, help me to cope.

My strength is spent; the journey's long.
My knees are weak; I can't go on.
But in my anguish and in my pain,
My Savior gently calls my name.

"I live in you, and we are one.
I'll lift your load when you're undone.
There's suffering here; I'll dry your tears.
I'm all you need; I am right here!"

"I've suffered much," He says to me.
"I paved the way to set you free.
I'll lift your load and take your cares.
Those broken dreams, I will repair.

I am sure-footed and know the way.
We'll walk and talk; We've much to say.
Just trust My lead and lean on Me.
I am the Way; I'm all you need."

"And my God will supply all your needs according to His riches in glory in Christ Jesus." Philippians 4:19 (NASB20)

"Jesus said to him, 'I am the way, and the truth, and the life; no one comes to the Father except through Me." John 14:6 (NASB20)

WALKING WITH JESUS

Tied up in knots,
All gnarled and twisted;
Out on a limb
Without any assistance.

Edging out further
And left all alone,
A choice I now face—

Do I risk going further
Or crawl off the limb
And quickly head back
To my comfort zone?

The thought of the warmth
And the fire inside
Is a pull that is strong
Where my fears could then hide,

But the further I edge
Out on that limb,
Where the sky is high
And the air is quite thin,
Comes a touch
From the Master
To calm fears within.

The noise from the crowds
And the people below
Is drowned out
By the Master
The higher I go.

'Cause walking with Jesus
And hearing His call
Far outweighs the risk
From the jeers of the crowd
And the mockers below.

The voice of the Master
And the love call within
Is the voice I now choose
As together we walk
Out on the edge of the limb.

"So do not fear, for I am with you; do not be dismayed, for I am your God. I will strengthen you and help you; I will uphold you with my righteous right hand." Isaiah 41:10 (NIV)

"Have I not commanded you? Be strong and courageous! Do not be terrified nor dismayed, for the Lord your God is with you wherever you go." Joshua 1:9 (NASB20)

YOU ARE REDEEMED

Chosen and called,
Blessed and redeemed.
Hand-picked by Me
And highly esteemed.

Favored among men
And called by My Name.
We are now one
And I took all your shame.

Created with purpose
And washed in My blood,
My chosen companion
And anointed in love.

The pride of My heart—
Redeemed and made new;
Blessed beyond measure
And always pursued.

Held in My hand
And molded by Me—
With purpose and favor,
Blessed and redeemed.

Fitted for glory
And wrapped in My love.
Now heaven-ready,
Straight from above.

Highly favored
And highly esteemed.
For you are My bride,
And you are redeemed!

"... so that Christ may dwell in your hearts through faith; and that you, being rooted and grounded in love, may be able to comprehend with all the saints what is the breadth and length and height and depth, and to know the love of Christ which surpasses knowledge, that you may be filled up to all the fullness of God." Ephesians 3:17-19 (NASB20)

YOU'LL BE OK

Not knowing what
Might lie ahead
Causes me to fear
And even dread.

But then I hear,
My child draw near.
Come sit with Me;
Pull up a chair.

My heart is yours,
So trust My hand.
I'll lead and guide;
That's who I Am.

I know just how to
Calm your fears;
That's what I do,
So just draw near.

Lean into Me;
Give me some time.
Your thoughts are rushed;
I will assign

A passage tried
And true will do
Down from the ages
But meant for you.

Give Me some time;
Digest My words.
My love wins out
That much is sure.

It's truth and grace
You need today;
I'll calm you down;
You'll be ok.

"Do not be anxious about anything, but in every situation, by prayer and petition, with thanksgiving, present your requests to God. And the peace of God, which transcends all understanding, will guard your hearts and your minds in Christ Jesus." Philippians 4:6-7 (NIV)

"When I am afraid, I will put my trust in You. In God, whose word I praise, In God I trust; I will not be afraid. What can mere mortals do to me?" Psalm 56:3-4 (NASB20)

YOUR TROUBLED HEART

Lay them down—
Those burdens—
Give them all to me.
Sit with Me awhile,
My child,
And I will set you free.

I am the Way, the Truth, the Life.
Your days are in My hands.
I'll meet Your needs,
Provide for you,
And calm your
Heart's demands.

Your thoughts
Are running wild,
My child,
So let Me slow your pace.
Look right at Me,
Sit for awhile,
And gaze into My face.

Before your day unfolds,
Put your busyness on hold.
Just let Me pour My love in you
Before your day ensues.

I am enough;
Give Me your fuss.
Give me your doubts and fears.
Let Me remind your troubled heart
That I am always here!

"Peace I leave you; My peace I give to you; not as the world gives, do I give to you. Do not let not your hearts be troubled, nor fearful." John 14:27 (NASB20)

"Jesus said to him, "I am the way, and the truth, and the life; no one comes to the Father except through Me." John 14:6 (NASB20)

HIS POWER

"Now to Him who is able to do far more abundantly beyond all that we ask or think, according to the power that works within us…"

Ephesians 3:20 (NASB20)

The power of Christ living in you is the same power that brought Jesus Christ back from the dead. Christ is IN you, and you are IN Christ:

> "To whom God willed to make known what is the wealth of the glory of this mystery among the Gentiles is, the mystery that is Christ in you, the hope of glory." Colossians 1:27 (NASB20)

> "I pray that the eyes of your heart may be enlightened, so that you will know what is the hope of His calling, what are the riches of the glory of His inheritance in the saints, and what is the boundless greatness of His power toward us who believe. These are in accordance with the working of the strength of His might which He brought about in Christ, when He raised Him from the dead and seated Him at His right hand in the heavenly places..." Ephesians 1:18-20 (NASB20)

There is power in the Name of Jesus! You now have the power to attack and defeat the enemy:

> "Behold, I have given you authority to tread on serpents and scorpions, and over all the power of the enemy, and nothing shall hurt you." Luke 10:19 (ESV)

Before you were saved, you were dead in your trespasses and sins:

> "As for you, you were dead in your transgressions and sins, in which you used to live when you followed the ways of this world and of the ruler of the kingdom of the air, the spirit who is now at work in those who are disobedient." Ephesians 2:1-2 (NIV)

Now you have His Power to walk in His good works:

> "For we are His workmanship, created in Christ Jesus for good works, which God prepared beforehand so that we would walk in them." Ephesians 2:10 (NASB20)

ANOINTED ONE

In this hour,
Before Christ comes,
He's searching out
To find that one

Who will take time
And sit with Him,
Bask in His love,
And listen in

To hear His voice
Above the noise,
To walk with Him
And make that choice.

We each are His
Anointed ones;
We have His Spirit;
We know God's Son.

The time is now;
The hour is late.
We are the Church;
We are His saints!

There's much at stake
At this late date,
But choose today
To stand up straight.

He longs for you
To embrace His heart,
To walk in Him
Right from the start

'Cause now's the time;
Lean into Him.
He wants to fill you
To the brim

So you'll spill out
On others' lives.
Then He can call them
His dear Bride!

"Now, it is God himself who has anointed us. And he is constantly strengthening both you and us in union with Christ. He knows we are his since he has also stamped his seal of love over our hearts and has given us the Holy Spirit like an engagement ring is given to a bride—a down payment of the blessings to come!" 2 Corinthians 1:21-22 (TPT)

A HEART OF WORSHIP

Spending time with God alone
Without your friends or your cell phone
Is precious time and is well-spent,
Costing only time, without a cent.

You worship Him with song and voice
And sense His presence above the noise.
You worship Him and praise His Name.
He's worth it all; He rules and reigns!

He sent His Word for us to know His will,
To meditate and just sit still,
To know the mind of Christ for you
As your mind and heart are renewed.

He points the way to know Him more
And helps you fight those inner wars.
The Word of God, you do adore.
You sense His will; you can't ignore.

You read His Word, and you dig deep
With other believers who also seek.
You are His saint; you're marching forth.
You're knocking down the enemy's doors!

"Be diligent to present yourself approved to God as a worker who does not need to be ashamed, accurately handling the word of truth." 2 Timothy 2:15 (NASB20)

"Finally, be strong in the Lord and in the strength of His might. Put on the full armor of God, so that you will be able to stand firm against the schemes of the devil. For our struggle is not against flesh and blood, but against the rulers, against the powers, against the world forces of this darkness, against the spiritual forces of wickedness in the heavenly places." Ephesians 6:10-12 (NASB20)

A ONE-MAN ACT

Thank you, Father,
For sending your Son.
My heart pours out;
I'm so undone!

You made a way;
You thought this through
So all mankind could
Talk to You.

You made a way
To enter in.
Jesus paid the price;
He took my sin.

He paid the price
For all mankind.
He did it once—
And for all time.

The Lamb was slain;
The blood was shed,
No rehearsal needed,
Sin put to bed.

He performed;
You wrote the script.
The veil was rent,
It was ripped

From top to bottom.
He made a way.
He gave His life.
He saved the day!

I'm privileged now.
I go backstage.
I boldly come
Before His face.

No need to rehearse
With line or verse.
He did it once
So we could have
A second birth.

Jesus saved the day;
I can't repay.
I humbly bow;
It's finished now.

The battle's won;
The stage was set.
A one-man act
With no regrets.

> "And behold, the veil of the temple was torn in two from top to bottom; and the earth shook and the rocks were split." Matthew 27:51 (NASB20)

> "For there is one God and one mediator between God and mankind, the man Christ Jesus..." 1 Timothy 2:5 (NIV)

> "Let us then with confidence draw near to the throne of grace, that we may receive mercy and find grace to help in time of need." Hebrews 4:16 (ESV)

ABANDONED TO YOU

Wrapped in Your love
And pulled close to You
For no one, no, never
Has loved like You do.

'Cause my heart overflows
As I'm abandoned to You
And praise just bursts forth
As my heart comes unglued.

Like the waves of the ocean
Pushing through,
I can count upon You
In all that You do.

Your assurance so true
As I'm abandoned to You
Is as sure and brand new
As the morning's fresh dew.

So praises will do
As I am learning to trust
And know without doubt
That You're always enough!

"Oh sing to the LORD a new song, for he has done marvelous things! His right hand and his holy arm have worked salvation for him." Psalm 98:1 (ESV)

"Make a joyful noise to the Lord, all the earth! Serve the Lord with gladness! Come into His presence with singing." Psalm 100:1-2 (ESV)

BUILDING FAITH

Swaying back and forth
Tick tock
Building faith
Against the clock.

Sitting still upon the Rock
And hearing Him
As others mock.

Holding fast
As others gasp
And clinging tight
Against the fright.

Being bold
While others hold
To sinking sand
And rubber bands.

Wanting Him
Above the rest.
He holds the time
And knows us best.

Spending time
With those who know
The Son of God
To help us grow.

Wrapped in Him
And holding tight.
We walk by faith
And not by sight.

Building faith
In Him alone
Is now to us
Our comfort zone.

"...for we walk by faith, not by sight..."
2 Corinthians 5:7 (NASB20)

"There is no one holy like the Lord, indeed, there is no one besides You, nor is there any rock like our God." 1 Samuel 2:2 (NASB20)

COURAGE COMES FROM YOU

Your ways seem so uncertain
For there's voices all around,
Pulling me away from You
With so many other sounds.

The subtlety of worldly things
That sparkle all around
Are causing me to draw away
But peace is nowhere found.

So then I choose to rest in You
And listen for Your voice.
You gently, oh so gently
Remind me of my choice.

So I choose to go Your way
And lean in above the noise;
To read Your Word and be with You
Then You cause me to rejoice.

You tell me to be strong in You
And in the power of Your Might;
To give my fear away to You
In the stillness of the night.

You remind me that You live in me;
To step out and trust Your lead,
And when I take that step with You,
You'll make me bold indeed!

That when I choose to trust You, Lord,
And not to be alarmed,
Your path will lead me
Straight to You,
Right into Your arms!

"Finally, be strong in the Lord and in the strength of His might." Ephesians 6:10 (NASB20)

FROM CARPENTER TO KING

He became man
Who walked with us
Down dusty roads,
And just because

He loved us so,
This Son of Man
Who bled and died
To take our hand.

A carpenter
Who took our shame,
Who died for us,
And knows our name.

A love so true
That makes us new,
His drops of blood
Were meant for you.

And now a King,
He took His place
By His Father's side
Near Heaven's gates.

He paid the price;
He can relate.
His return is near;
He won't be late.

He's coming back;
He bridged the gap.
He paid the time;
He took our wrath.

A carpenter
And yet a King
Who shed His blood
Now rules and reigns!

"'Is not this the carpenter, the son of Mary and brother of James and Joses and Judas and Simon? And are not his sisters here with us?' And they took offense at Him. And Jesus said to them, 'A prophet is not without honor, except in his hometown and among his relatives and in his own household.'" Mark 6:3-4 (ESV)

"These will wage war against the Lamb, and the Lamb will overcome them because He is Lord of lords and King of kings; and those who are with Him are the called and chosen and faithful." Revelation 17:14 (NASB20)

HIS PRECIOUS BLOOD

Fellowship was on His heart;
God had a plan right from the start.
A brand new nature He would give
And make us ready to one day live

With Him in heaven was God's own plan.
God sent His Son to buy back man,
To pay the price with His own blood,
Now heaven-ready, straight from above.

A brand-new nature, you now are one;
You have His Life, the Risen Son.
He paid the price; He's been your High Priest
Since the hour you first believed.

So when the enemy taunts you so
And accuses you, just let him know
That you're redeemed and set apart
With Christ's own blood, He did impart.

And then remind him no guilt is found,
That you're set free, no longer bound.
You are redeemed, bought with a price.
Jesus paid for your sins with His own life.

The work is done; it's finished now.
His blood was shed; we humbly bow,
For now we know His love so true
When His own blood was shed for you!

The blood of bulls or goats won't do,
But Jesus' blood did rescue you.
He made a way to set you free:
The blood He shed on Calvary!

"But in those sacrifices there is a reminder of sins every year. For it is impossible for the blood of bulls and goats to take away sins." Hebrews 10:3-4 (NASB20)

"But now in Christ Jesus you who previously were far away have been brought near by the blood of Christ..." Ephesians 2:13 (NASB20)

I'M CALLING YOU

No longer will you straddle
That fence that's in the way;
I'm calling you, today, My child,
To be bold and unafraid.

Just listen for My voice within
And come and follow Me.
I'll lead the way; I am the Way.
Just trust Me and believe.

Please know that we are One
When you asked me in your heart.
You'll sense My gentle nudge
As together we'll embark.

I promise to provide for you;
You are My treasured bride.
My heart is yours; I'm here for you.
I'll be your loving guide.

Just rest upon My chest, My child
And believe My plans are best.
We'll run through valleys and meadows;
I'll show you plans for what's ahead.

I have anointed and appointed you
For a work that we will do.
When you sit with Me and glean from Me,
You'll be strengthened and renewed!

"Have I not commanded you? Be strong and courageous! Do not be terrified nor dismayed, for the LORD your God is with you wherever you go." Joshua 1:9 (NASB20)

"And this is my prayer: that your love may abound more and more in knowledge and depth of insight, so that you may be able to discern what is best and may be pure and blameless for the day of Christ, filled with the fruit of righteousness that comes through Jesus Christ—to the glory and praise of God." Philippians 1:9-11 (NIV)

LIGHT AND LIFE

Light and life
Are in Your hands.
You've made the heavens
And grains of sand.

You've spoken light
And made the day.
You've placed the sun
And made it stay
Up in the sky
So far away.

You brought hope
When there was none.
You sent your Son
For everyone.

You tasted death
For just a while.
You took our sin
And walked our mile.

You light our path
And You're the Way.
You are our Life
For each new day.

"For with you is the fountain of life; in your light we see light." Psalm 36:9 (NIV)

"Jesus said to him, 'I am the way, and the truth, and the life; no one comes to the Father except through Me.'" John 14:6 (NASB20)

"It was now about noon, and darkness came over the whole land until three in the afternoon, for the sun stopped shining. And the curtain of the temple was torn in two. Jesus called out with a loud voice, 'Father, into your hands I commit my spirit.' When he had said this, he breathed his last." Luke 23:44-46 (NIV)

OUT AMONGST THE WOLVES

The Savior of your soul
Has come to make you whole.
He'll make you unafraid
And calm your fears today.

Out amongst the wolves
He will send you with His Word.
He'll light the path for you
In all you say and do.

Your weakness He will use,
So move out without excuse.
He'll make you strong in Him
When you're thrust out on a limb.

He'll calm you down inside
So choose to just abide.
Then give Him all your fears
Who will dry up all your tears.

Speak with truth and love
And be as gentle as a dove.
Just trust His plans for you,
And He will see you through.

He'll send you to the crowd;
To the humble and the proud,
His messenger is you
'Cause they need a Savior, too!

"'You are my witnesses,' declares the LORD, 'and my servant whom I have chosen, so that you may know and believe me and understand that I am he.'" Isaiah 43:10a (NIV)

"Behold, I am sending you out as sheep in the midst of wolves, so be wise as serpents and innocent as doves." Matthew 10:16 (ESV)

STEP OUT IN THE LIGHT

Bound up by fear
And afraid to step out,
You're all out of sorts
And captured by doubt,

Groping in darkness
And filled with despair
But sensing His calling
To step out in fresh air.

The fairest Lord Jesus,
The Ruler of All,
Is the Light of the World,
So you can stand tall!

There's healing in Him,
And you are His voice.
It's a new day for you
With anointing and choice.

For you are redeemed,
And He's calling your name.
There's blessing and purpose
"Cause you carry His flame.

So yield to His leading
For He leads from within.
He'll take all your fears,
And new trust will begin.

Just yield to His will
And believe He knows best
As He shines from within
To bring hope and bring rest.

"Again Jesus spoke to them, saying, 'I am the light of the world. Whoever follows me will not walk in darkness, but will have the light of life.'" John 8:12 (ESV)

"In the same way, let your light shine before others, that they may see your good deeds and glorify your Father in heaven." Matthew 5:16 (NIV)

"Your word is a lamp for my feet, a light on my path." Psalms 119:105 (NIV)

THE TIME IS NOW

The time is now;
This is the hour,
No time to fret
Or have regrets.

The hour is late;
Don't hesitate.
He needs your "yes;"
He'll do the rest.

You are His choice
To be His voice.
He'll light your fire
With His desires.

He'll make you bold
As plans unfold.
The Christ in you
Will see you through.

He is the spark
Out in the dark.
He'll light the way;
He is the Way.

You are His flame
Where hope remains
The Christ in you
For others, too!

"For he says, 'In the time of my favor I heard you, and in the day of salvation I helped you.' I tell you, now is the time of God's favor, now is the day of salvation." 2 Corinthians 6:2 (NIV)

"'You are my witnesses,' declares the LORD, 'and my servant whom I have chosen, that you may know and believe me and understand that I am he. Before me no god was formed, nor shall there be any after me.'" Isaiah 43:10 (ESV)

TRUST HIS STEPS

When faced with deep despair
And wondering who is there,
Just bow your head and say a prayer
And trust the God who cares.

When you are weak and need His touch,
Just call on Him to fill you up.
He'll strengthen you in ways unknown
When you feel down and all alone.

He'll meet your needs;
He knows your pain.
He'll strengthen you
When you feel drained.

Sometimes He'll use a special tool.
He'll send a friend to be the fuel
To encourage you along the way
And help you face another day.

He is your Life and knows you best.
His love will lead, so trust the rest.
He'll undergird and give you hope
When you are weak and cannot cope.

He'll take your weakness and lead within
So trust His steps where strength begins.

"But he answered me, 'My grace is always more than enough for you, and my power finds its full expression through your weakness.' So I will celebrate my weaknesses, for when I'm weak I sense more deeply the mighty power of Christ living in me. So I'm not defeated by my weakness, but delighted! For when I feel my weakness and endure mistreatment—when I'm surrounded with troubles on every side and face persecution because of my love for Christ—I am made yet stronger. For my weakness becomes a portal to God's power." 2 Corinthians 12:9-10 (TPT)

WALK IN HIS PLAN

Hidden beneath
The rubble of life
Where death had a grip
With all kinds of strife,

Then Jesus' strong arm
Lifted you out
Of the muck and the mire,
Out of fears and your doubts.

He reached out His hand
And showed you your sin;
He gave you His life,
And you're now born again.

You're joined to the Savior;
You're in union with Him.
You live, and you move,
And you're new from within.

He is the path
Because He is the Way,
So lean into His lead
For all of your days.

As your mind is renewed
And you know whose you are,
You'll co-labor with Christ
And follow the Star.

His Presence and Glory
Will now be your story
As you walk in His plan
With the Great, "I AM!"

"For we are God's fellow workers. You are God's field, God's building." 1 Corinthians 3:9 (ESV)

"Jesus said to him, 'I am the way, and the truth, and the life; no one comes to the Father except through Me.'" John 14:6 (NASB20)

"Have I not commanded you? Be strong and courageous! Do not be terrified or dismayed, for the Lord your God is with you wherever you go." Joshua 1:9 (NASB20)

WRAPPED IN RIGHTEOUSNESS

Surely, oh surely,
This cannot be so—
That Jesus became sin,
And yet did you know

Not even a speck
Of debt did He owe,
So pure and so holy
Like white, driven snow,

This incarnate One
Sent down from above
Who died in our place;
Now the work has been done.

New Life we are given,
And we become one—
When we come to the cross
And believe on His Son.

He gives us Himself
And His righteousness, too.
Yes, it could be—
Yes, it is true:

Jesus paid the price
For me and for you.
We are wrapped and secure
In His blanket of love.
We are now heaven-ready;
We're redeemed by His blood!

"For our sake he made him to be sin who knew no sin, so that in him we might become the righteousness of God." 2 Corinthians 5:21 (ESV)

"But the one who joins himself to the Lord is mingled into one spirit with him." 1 Corinthians 6:17 (TPT)

"I will rejoice greatly in the Lord, My soul will be joyful in my God; for He has clothed me with garments of salvation, He has wrapped me with a robe of righteousness, as a groom puts on a turban, and as a bride adorns herself with her jewels." Isaiah 61:10 (NASB20)

WRAPPED IN SCANDAL

The truth, (can you handle?)
Was wrapped in such scandal.
The gossip did spread
As the shepherds were led

To a babe in a manger
In a stable near strangers.
A virgin gave birth
So God could be with us
Down here on earth.

The Name above all names
Was given to Him:
They named him Jesus.
He would die for our sins.

The news, it got out,
And the scandal did spread
Because Jesus was healing
And raising the dead.

And a new day was here
And new Life we could find
Where we would be known
As one of a kind!

We'd be loved by the One
Who the scandal was after;
The One they made fun of
With the jeers and the laughter.

And then came the time
When Jesus died on that tree;
He died in our place
For you and for me.

For God, who is holy
And can't look upon sin,
Sent His spotless Lamb
So we could know Him
And have peace within.

We'd be wrapped in His grace
And then be assigned
A place in heaven
And not left behind.

Oh, such scandalous love
Sent down from above,
Who would walk to the cross
And suffer such loss

And die in our place
And be placed in a grave
And rise from the dead.
Oh, what more could we say,

But worship the One
That was wrongly accused,
Who took such abuse
For me and for you!

REFELCTIONS AFTER A SERMON BY PASTOR RICK ATCHLEY

"But I tell you, love your enemies and pray for those who persecute you." Matthew 5:44 (NIV)

YOU WILL SEE

Life will look different;
I'm changing your plans.
I now live inside;
I'm the Great, "I AM!"

You're My Masterpiece, child,
And your Life is in Me.
I'll bring joy and new hope;
Oh, you'll see, you will see!

I'll not turn away;
I'm now here to stay.
You're made in My image,
And your sin has been paid.

I'm the Lamb who was slain;
I'm the Ancient of Days.
You asked Me in,
And I'm now here to stay.

So stop striving; just rest
And believe I know best.
There's new freedom in Me.
Oh, you'll see, you will see!

And when the storms brew
And you've not a clue what to do,
I'll turn the tide,
Or I'll walk through with you.

As we walk through new doors,
Let My hand be in yours,
For you're sufficient in Me;
Oh, you'll see; you will see!

"I pray that the eyes of your heart may be enlightened so that you will know what is the hope of His calling, what are the riches of the glory of His inheritance in the saints, and what is the boundless greatness of His power toward us who believe." Ephesians 1:18-19a (NASB20)

HIS PRAISE

"It is good to give thanks to the Lord, to sing praises to Your name, O Most High; to declare Your steadfast love in the morning and Your faithfulness at night…"

Psalm 92:1-2 (ESV)

This Praise chapter is a very personal one to me because I had never known spiritual attacks like I have experienced while in the process of writing a book. The enemy certainly did not want me to bring glory to God in any way, but I have found the warfare has been especially intense during this season of my life. My poem, "Join the Choir," was birthed out of my struggles.

However, God has had me praising Him in song in the mornings, and I have found that praise drives the enemy away. I have discovered there is victory in learning to praise the Lord as well as, of course, praying and studying the Word of God:

> "Let everything that has breath praise the Lord. Praise the Lord!" Psalm 150:6 (NIV)

God is omnipresent – everywhere, but His presence is especially intense in an atmosphere of praise:

> "Yet you are holy, enthroned upon the praises of Israel." Psalm 22:3 (ESV)

> "To grant those who mourn in Zion, giving them a garland instead of ashes, the oil of gladness instead of mourning, the cloak of praise instead of a disheartened spirit..." Isaiah 61:3 (NASB20)

> "In God, whose word I praise, in the Lord, whose word I praise, in God I have put my trust, I shall not be afraid. What can mankind do to me? Your vows are binding upon me, God; I will render thanksgiving offerings to You. For You have saved my soul from death, indeed my feet from stumbling, so that I may walk before God in the light of the living." Psalm 56:10-13 (NASB20)

Worshiping God reminds us that HE IS GOD and that WE ARE HIS PEOPLE.

HE IS WORTHY OF ALL OUR PRAISE!

ENAMORED BY LOVE

Enamored by love
Oh, the depth of the cross
And the blood that was shed
At such a high cost.

Enamored by love
Was the focus You kept
While You stayed in the garden
As you prayed and You wept.

Enamored by love
As You died for all men
When You hung on that cross
And paid for man's sin.

Enamored by love
As your body was torn
So we would know You
As You carried the scorn.

Enamored by love
Oh, the price has been paid
For You said it was finished
On that glorious day.

Enamored by love
When You rose from the dead
As we rose with you, too
Just like your Word says.

Enamored by love
Out of death to New Life
Was the gift that You gave
For the love of your Bride!

"But God demonstrates his own love for us in this: While we were still sinners, Christ died for us." Romans 5:8 (NIV)

"See how great a love the Father has given us, that we would be called children of God; and in fact we are. For this reason the world does not know us: because it did not know Him." 1 John 3:1 (NASB20)

GOD WITH US

An ancient plan
God's gift to man
To give us His Son
His only one!

A spotless Lamb
To redeem back man
So we'd know Him
He'd take our sin.

He made a fuss
He handed us
The best He had
This little lad.

His only Son
The incarnate One
Down from above
And wrapped in love.

This "God with us"
Who is enough
Who is our Life
Our guiding light.

He found us lost
He paid the cost
Sent down to man
The Great "I Am!"

So we'd know Him
He'd live within
He'd walk with us
And call us friend!

"... She will give birth to a son and will call him Immanuel (which means 'God is with us')." Isaiah 7:14 (NLT)

"Never will I leave you; never will I forsake you." Hebrews 13:5 (NIV)

JOIN THE CHOIR

Learn to praise Him;
Grab a song.
Join the choir;
Sing along.

Come find your voice
Above the noise
To sing and shout
And praise it out.

When darkest shadows
Fill your space,
You've fallen flat
Upon your face,

When life's not fair,
You're in despair,
Just pull away
And find somewhere

To grab a song
And find a mic
Then watch the enemy
Take a hike.

"Cause what you've done
Is praise the Son
Who deserves your praise
For all your days.

You've called upon
The One so true;
By praising Him
Brings your rescue.

So join the choir
And find a song
'Cause praising Him
Was what you needed
All along!

FIRST PUBLISHED IN *ALL MY DESIRE*, 2023

"To all who mourn in Israel, he will give a crown of beauty for ashes, a joyous blessing instead of mourning, festive praise instead of despair." Isaiah 61:3a (NLT)

"I will praise the name of God with a song; I will magnify him with thanksgiving." Psalm 69:30 (ESV)

MY HOPE AND REST

Standing still
And crushed from life;
Filled with rage
And raw from strife.

A valley gnarled
With tangled mess;
Scars have formed
Along with stress.

Muck and mire
Echoes back.
Where are you, Lord?
A chasm deep
That speaks of lack.

But eyes were blind—
I looked away;
Your love runs deep—
It's here to stay.

I looked outside;
You live within.
My peace is You,
My joy begins

To settle me
And calm me down;
I've looked outside
And all around.

I'm one with You—
I've always been
Since You came in
And took my sin.

Though outward signs
May still abound,
When tossed about
And thunder sounds,

Yet, still my peace
And hope's in view
I'm learning now
To cling to You.

A new day dawns;
New hope runs deep.
My anchor holds,
Now I can sleep.

I trust Your plan;
You know what's best.
You are my peace
And hope and rest!

"You keep him in perfect peace whose mind is stayed on you, because he trusts in you." Isaiah 26:3 (ESV)

"...rejoicing in hope, persevering in tribulation, devoted to prayer..." Romans 12:12 (NASB20)

"Come to me, all of you who are weary and carry heavy burdens, and I will give you rest." Matthew 11:28 (NLT)

MY TIME

A time to sit
A time to pray
A time to put
All else away.

A time to lay
All else aside
A time to let Him
Lead and guide.

A time to hear
His voice so clear
To hear Him speak
With heart and ear.

A time to rest
And let Him speak
For He is strong
And I am weak.

A time to lean
And give Him time
To know His love
For me is mine.

A time to know
Right from the start
When Jesus whispers
To my heart.

Just Him and I
This time I seek
To know His love
Makes me complete!

"Be still, and know that I am God. . ." Psalm 46:10 (NLT)

OUR VOICES RAISED

In the silence of the morning,
When the dew is on the ground,
The birds are calling forth God's glory,
And with their voices they resound.

They're echoing His goodness
As the morning makes its way,
And the sun is shining brightly
With brilliant colors on display.

The serenading choir,
All sitting on a wire,
Ushers in a song of love,
With raised voices just like a dove.

I listened to the choir
Where no hymnal was required.
I just sensed that they've been heard
Amongst the choir of the birds.
No tenors or sopranos
Or the sound of grand pianos
Were heard amongst the birds.
Just a melody was ringing
Without a spoken word.

They had no care or worry,
Nor were they in a hurry.
They were free to raise their voices
With chattering melodies and noises.

There's a lesson to be learned
Amongst the choir of the birds.
We learn to praise our Savior
Because we've each found favor.

He will lead you to that wire,
Where you'll have a deep desire,
To sing His praise all of your days
And sing amongst the choir!

"Sing to Him, sing praises to Him; Tell of all His wonders." Psalm 105:2 (NASB20)

"I will tell of your name to my brothers; in the midst of the congregation I will sing your praise." Hebrews 2:12 (ESV)

YOU ARE ENOUGH

Delight in Me
And know My ways.
Come go with Me;
It's a brand new day.

So walk with Me;
I'm not back there.
Just focus, child,
And be aware.

There's more ahead;
The day is new.
Give up the past;
There's work to do.

Just listen close
And heed My call.
You will not hear
Unless you fall

Into My arms
And carve out time,
So sit with me;
I will remind

You that we're one;
Just you and Me.
The world will change;
Just let it be.

But You and I,
We are a team.
I'll be your strength;
Your everything.

I love you, child;
You're set apart
To know My ways
Then you'll impart

A glimpse of hope
In others' lives.
I'll point the way;
We'll sacrifice.

We'll find that one
Who needs My touch.
Come go with Me;
You are enough.

> "For in Him all the fullness of Deity dwells in bodily form, and in Him you have been made complete, and He is the head over every ruler and authority." Colossians 2:9-10 (NASB20)

> "He made Him who knew no sin to be sin on our behalf, so that we might become the righteousness of God in Him." 2 Corinthians 5:21 (NASB20)

YOU'RE MY SONG

Time comes crashing to the shore.
There's much to do outside my door,
But, as I choose to know You more,
Your voice is clear above the roar.

Though storm clouds loom
And fears abound,
I sense Your peace;
You calm me down.

Jesus, precious friend of mine,
That's where I choose
To feast and dine

Upon Your love as I recline
And know You more
As You remind
Me that I belong
'Cause You're my song.

I'll sing it loud
Above the crowd
And tell the world
They need you now.

You're one with Me.
We're tried and true.
I pull away
And talk to You.

You hold my hand
And let me know
It's almost time
That we should go.

We'll walk outside;
I'll hum Your tune
So others know
There's always room

For just one more.
He died for you,
'Cause You're the one
He's searching for!

"For I am not ashamed of the gospel, for it is the power of God for salvation to everyone who believes, to the Jew first and also to the Greek." Romans 1:16-17 (NASB20)

"'You are My witnesses,' declares the Lord, 'And My servant whom I have chosen, so that you may know and believe Me and understand that I am He...'" Isaiah 43:10 (NASB20)

HIS PRESENCE

"And He said, 'My presence shall go with you, and I will give you rest.'"

Exodus 33:14 (NASB20)

We are His children, and He promises to never leave us or forsake us. We are in a love relationship with the Father.

In the Old Testament, the Holy Spirit came "upon" a person and briefly empowered individuals. King David pleaded that the Holy Spirit not be taken from him after he had sinned in having sexual relations with Bathsheba. The Holy Spirit did not permanently dwell in the Old Testament saints:

> "Do not cast me away from Your presence and do not take your Holy Spirit from me." Psalm 51:11 (NASB20)

The Holy Spirit's ministry to believers changed after Christ's death and resurrection. Jesus prophesied many times that the Holy Spirit would come:

> "And behold, I am sending the promise of My Father upon you; but you are to stay in the city until you are clothed with power from on high." Luke 24:49 (NASB20)

> "Nevertheless, I tell you the truth: it is to your advantage that I go away, for if I do not go away, the Helper will not come to you. But if I go, I will send him to you." John 16:7 (ESV)

The Holy Spirit now indwells believers:

> "In Him, you also, after listening to the message of truth, the gospel of your salvation—having also believed, you were sealed in Him with the Holy Spirit of promise..." Ephesians 1:13 (NASB20)

UNDER THE OLD COVENANT, GOD CAME TO VISIT. UNDER THE NEW COVENANT, HE MOVED IN.

A BLAZING SURRENDER

Nothing compares to Your love,
This I know;
To sit in Your Presence
With my heart all aglow.

You have my attention;
You pour out Your grace.
You wrap me in love
As I echo Your praise.

Your acceptance so true,
For You've made me brand new.
You are worthy of honor
In all that You do.

My burdens are hushed
With the brush of Your love,
As You steady my cares
For I know You're enough.

Then when I walk onward
And step into my day,
The glow from Your Glory
Will help guide my way.

For Your love spurs me onward
To share Your great Name,
In a blazing surrender
As I carry Your flame!

"But you will receive power when the Holy Spirit comes on you; and you will be my witnesses in Jerusalem, and in all Judea and Samaria, and to the ends of the earth." Acts 1:8 (NIV)

"How lovely is your dwelling place, O Lord of hosts! My soul longs, yes, faints for the courts of the Lord; my heart and my flesh sing for joy to the living God." Psalm 84:1-2 (ESV)

"Therefore, if anyone is in Christ, he is a new creation. The old has passed away; behold, the new has come." 2 Corinthians 5:17 (ESV)

A SPITTIN' IMAGE

A spittin' image
Of the Son.
There is no doubt
You know the One

Who died for you
And paid the price
To set you free—
You've sacrificed.

Turn to the side;
You look like Him.
You reflect His love
Straight from above.

No need to guess;
You know His Name,
'Cause it's so plain
You carry His flame.

You walk in grace
And not the law;
Yet truth wins out
Above it all.

You count the cost
And know the loss
But cling to Him
When you are tossed
To and fro.

You don't skirt the cross
But walk right through.
You lean on Him
In all you do.

You've known pain
And suffering, too,
Yet now His scars
Shine bright on you.

You're a spittin' image;
So plain to see.
You reflect the Son
Who's set you free!

> "But we all, with unveiled faces, looking as in a mirror at the glory of the Lord, are being transformed into the same image from glory to glory, just as from the Lord, the Spirit." 2 Corinthians 3:18 (NASB20)

BLENDED LIVES

A blended life
Now we are one—
A reflected love
From heaven above.

No longer separate
And all alone.
When He came in,
He found a home.

He settled down
And made a way.
We now are one—
Not far away.

Christ in me
And me in Him.
Our love runs deep—
I am complete.

We walk and talk;
I read His Word.
He listens well;
My heart is stirred.

A passage tried
And true for me.
Our blended lives;
He helps me see

Which way to go;
This life we live—
He shows me how
To then forgive.

This flaming One
That lives in me;
He lights my way
'Cause He's the Way.

My comfort zone—
Not all alone.
My friend for life—
He sacrificed

His life for me—
Now blended in.
And set apart—
He took my sin.

He's made a way
Into my heart.
Such hope for me
Right from the start!

> "The glory which You have given Me I also have given to them, so that they may be one, just as We are one; I in them and You in Me, that they may be perfected in unity, so that the world may know that You sent Me, and You loved them, just as You loved Me." John 17:22-23 (NASB20)

DYNAMIC DUO

Dynamic Duo
You and me.
You made me righteous;
You set me free.

I come boldly
To Your throne
With fearless joy,
I call your phone.

You're never busy;
You're always there.
You live in me;
Your love we share.

You know my hurts;
You know my cares.
You hold me tight;
We're quite a pair!

Dynamic Duo
The two of us;
You are the Way;
You made a fuss.

You sealed the deal;
You became sin.
You made a way
To enter in.

Dynamic Duo
We walk this earth.
You've given me
A second birth.

The blood You shed,
The price you paid—
This was God's plan,
The only way.

You rose again
Without delay;
Your righteousness
You gave away

So I would say
I can't repay
But humbly bow
To You each day.

Dynamic Duo
Oh could it be;
That You would choose
To live in me!

"But the one who joins himself to the Lord is one spirit with Him." 1 Corinthians 6:17 (NASB20)

"For God made the only one who did not know sin to become sin for us, so that we might become the righteousness of God through our union with Him." 2 Corinthians 5:21 (TPT)

ENJOYING HIS PRESENCE

I'm enjoying your Presence
And know You are mine.
I sit with you, Jesus;
Your love is divine.

You walk with me, Jesus;
You live in my heart.
I relax in your love
Which will never depart.

You paid the price
For all of my sin,
And because of
Such love,
You now call me friend.

So my answer is,
"Yes, Lord,
I yield to your love.
You're the light
Of the world,
And you're
Always enough."

Now I answer your call
And listen for You
'Cause your plan is best
In all that You do.

Oh, could it be so
That I'm sealed in your love
And you've paved the way
For my home up above!

"And so, dear brothers and sisters, we can boldly enter heaven's Most Holy Place because of the blood of Jesus." Hebrews 10:19 (NLT)

"But our citizenship is in heaven. And we eagerly await a Savior from there, the Lord Jesus Christ..." Philippians 3:20 (NIV)

GUARD YOUR HEART

Darkness is looming
All over the earth,
So don't be distracted
For worldly pleasures
Will surely hurt

Your witness of Him
When you stumble and sin,
When you follow the world
In the midst of a whim.

Don't open the door
And let darkness in.
Don't linger too long;
That will lure you to sin.

Darkness is looming
So guard your heart;
Worldly pleasures
Were here from the start.

Look straight ahead
And follow the One
Who knows the path
That will lead you home.

His name is Jesus.
He's the Light of the World.
He knows the way
Because He is the Way.

He lives inside you,
And now you are one;
So rest in His love
And follow the Son!

"Watch over your heart with all diligence, for from it flow the springs of life. Rid yourself of a deceitful mouth and keep devious speech far from you. Let your eyes look directly ahead and let your gaze be fixed straight in front of you. Watch the path of your feet, and all your ways will be established." Proverbs 4:23-26 (NASB20)

HE SATISFIES

Gazing deeply
Along the brook
To watch and pray
And take a look,

To find that cranny,
To find that nook,
To know Him more,
To read His book

And be with Him:
It is my choice
To listen closely
For His voice.

I come so boldly
Because I can.
He told me to—
This Great, "I Am."

He lives in me,
And we are one.
He speaks to me,
Leaves me undone.

Oh, what a Savior,
What a friend.
I meet Him there
And He does send
His love to me
Which will not end.

His secrets,
He does share with me
When I spend time
Upon His knee

To know Him more
To hear Him say,
"Come sit with Me.
Give Me your day."

Oh Jesus,
Gentle friend of mine,
When I forget,
You do remind

Me not just once,
But many times,
That I belong
Even when I'm wrong.

He said, "it's finished."
He paid the price.
I sit with Him;
He does supply.

He sends His love
It's He and I
For nothing else
Now satisfies!

> "You make known to me the path of life; in Your presence is fullness of joy..." Psalm 16:11 (ESV)

> "Jesus answered and said to her, "Everyone who drinks of this water will be thirsty again; but whoever drinks of the water that I will give him shall never be thirsty; but the water that I will give him will become in him a fountain of water springing up to eternal life." John 4:13-14 (NASB20)

HIGHLY FAVORED

Spend some time with Him today;
Give Him your "yes" without delay.
Believe He loves you; this is true.
Come sit with Him; He lives in you.

You're highly favored and set apart;
He knows your name; He has your heart.
Just like Mary, He called her name
Without fortune and without fame.

She said "yes" when called upon
To be the mother of the incarnate One;
The chosen one to carry the Son
To redeem the world for everyone.

She suffered loss, but she said "yes;"
She was chosen above the rest.
She suffered much along the way;
The soldiers carried Him away.

She watched Him die on that Friday.
Her soul was pierced; she was dismayed.
But oh, the joy when He appeared
To her that day; He took her fear.

And you are called; you're set apart.
You're highly favored; you have a part
To advance the Kingdom here on earth
So others have a second birth.

Just be that one who will say "yes"
And hear His call above the rest.
You're highly favored and loved by Him.
He died for you; He took your sin.

You're set apart; you're one with Him.
He loves you so; He calls you friend.
He'll walk with you; He is enough.
His love will lead; that's what He does!

"And coming in, he said to her, 'Greetings, O favored one, the Lord is with you! ... Do not be afraid, Mary, for you have found favor with God.'" Luke 1:28, 30 (NASB20)

"For whoever finds me finds life and receives favor from the LORD." Proverbs 8:35 (NLT)

JOINED TO JESUS

Joined to Jesus:
Oh, yes it's true;
The cross did work
For me and you.

Joined to Jesus:
There's union now;
Sins paid in full,
We humbly bow.

Joined to Jesus:
The old has gone,
A brand-new heart,
A brand-new song.

Joined to Jesus:
Walk in His grace;
With eyes on Him,
We run the race.

Joined to Jesus:
He set you free;
He gave you Life,
His liberty!

Joined to Jesus:
Your debt's been paid,
No longer lost,
But now you're saved.

Joined to Jesus:
From east to west
Your sins removed
Such blessedness!

"The LORD is compassionate and gracious, slow to anger, abounding in love. He will not always accuse, nor will he harbor his anger forever; he does not treat us as our sins deserve or repay us according to our iniquities. For as high as the heavens are above the earth, so great is his love for those who fear him; as far as the east is from the west, so far has he removed our transgressions from us." Psalm 103: 8-12 (NIV)

LEFT BEHIND

Left behind memories,
Left behind dust,
In a struggle to leave,
In the midst of the rush.

Left behind friends,
Left behind trash,
Left behind flowers,
And accumulated cash.

I grab my coat and
My scarf and my gloves
But because we are One,
I'm wrapped in Your love.

There's assurance so true
As I shut the front door;
We walk out together
'Cause it's You I adore.

I'm clothed in Your Presence;
You're my Master within.
We will face future days
Because You are my friend.

'Cause one thing's for sure
In each season of time.
We do life together;
I don't leave You behind.

"To them God chose to make known how great among the Gentiles are the riches of the glory of this mystery, which is Christ in you, the hope of glory." Colossians 1:27 (ESV)

"Listen to me, descendants of Jacob, all you who remain in Israel. I have cared for you since you were born. Yes, I carried you before you were born. I will be your God throughout your lifetime—until your hair is white with age. I made you, and I will care for you. I will carry you along and save you." Isaiah 46:3-4 (NLT)

NAIL-SCARRED HANDS

Reach out your hand
And give in to His plan.
Jesus reached out to you
With His nail-scarred hands.

He made a way
To say yes to your day
So hand over to Him
Your fears from within.

The sorrow and loss
That He bore on that cross
And the nails in His hands
As He died for all men.

The scars that He bore
And the love that He wore
When He suffered and bled
As He put sin to bed.

Bleeding and raw
Yet in the future, He saw
The sins of all men
He paid for back then

Out of death
He brought life
So with hands lifted high
We can praise His dear Name
Without any shame.

Oh, how could we not
But be undone by the cost
And place in His hands
What we don't understand.

So give Him your "yes,"
And He'll take care the rest
'Cause He carried your shame
With His wonderful Name!

"And it was the third hour when they crucified Him." Mark 15:25 (ESV)

"Then he said to Thomas, 'Put your finger here, and see my hands; and put out your hand, and place it in my side. Do not disbelieve, but believe.' Thomas answered him, 'My Lord and my God!' Jesus said to him, 'Have you believed because you have seen me? Blessed are those who have not seen and yet have believed.'" John 20: 27-29 (ESV)

PLACED IN GRACE

Sitting in Your love
And basking in Your grace
Straight from up above
As I gaze into Your face

"Come, child of Mine,"
He whispers to my heart.
He says, "Come sit with Me—
I've loved you from the start.

Don't think you have to hide;
My arms are open wide.
Come boldly to My throne;
My heart is now your home.

This is a brand-new day.
Your sins were washed away.
Oh weary one of mine,
Come sit and spend some time.

My grace is freely given
Because you are forgiven.
Come talk with Me today;
I've got so much to say.

So come and take My hand.
I am the Great, 'I Am!'
Come fellowship with Me;
I died to set you free!"

"For from His fullness we have all received, and grace upon grace." John 1:16 (ESV)

"Let us then with confidence draw near to the throne of grace, that we may receive mercy and find grace to help in time of need." Hebrews 4:16 (ESV)

PULLING BACK THE CURTAIN

Pulling back the curtain,
Exposing all the lies,
'Cause now I'm learning
Whose I am and why
He had to die.

I died with Him that day
On that cross so long ago.
He bled and died
And rose again
So I could get to know

The Son of God,
That One alone,
Who died and rose again.
The work is finished;
He paid the price
And took away my sin.

His grace is free;
This much is sure,
But grace is never cheap
'Cause resting in His finished work
Takes the pressure off of me.

When for so long
I worked for Him
And thought I did my best,
But I never learned to walk in Him
And lean upon His chest.

So exposing all the lies
And learning how to rest
Is letting go and letting God
And not performing at my best.

'Cause pulling back the curtain
From fleshly patterns in the way
Means learning how to
Walk in Him and let Him
Take my day.

REFLECTIONS AFTER A TEACHING BY FRANK FRIEDMANN

> "Now if we died with Christ, we believe that we will also live with Him." Romans 6:8 (NIV)

> "So I say, let the Holy Spirit guide your lives. Then you won't be doing what your sinful nature craves. The sinful nature wants to do evil, which is just the opposite of what the Spirit wants. And the Spirit gives us desires that are the opposite of what the sinful nature desires. These two forces are constantly fighting each other, so you are not free to carry out your good intentions." Galatians 5:16-17 (NLT)

REKINDLE ANEW

Rekindle anew
What was given to you.
No time to look back on
Those regrets of the past.

It's a new day in Me,
So trust and believe.
We've new mountains to climb—
I'll not leave you behind.

So give Me your all
When you stumble and fall.
I am your Life
With no worry or strife.

My companion, my friend,
It's a new day; lean in.
It's time to press on—
Let's sing a new song!

Rekindle anew
The flame that's in you,
For I've set you apart
Right from the start.

You are My choice,
And you are My voice
To proclaim My great Name
'Cause you carry My flame!

"For this reason I remind you to fan into flame the gift of God, which is in you through the laying on of my hands. For the Spirit God gave us does not make us timid, but gives us power, love and self-discipline." 2 Timothy 1:6-7 (NIV)

STEPPIN' OUT AND STEPPIN' IN

Once upon a time ago, the Savior came
And made you whole.

For many years you worked for Him
And thought that helped to cover sin.
You lost your joy; your passion waned.
You wondered if His love remained.

And then one day you heard the news:
He took your sin and made you new.
You are in Christ; you're new within.
Now you're steppin' out and steppin' in.

Steppin' out from guilt and shame
And steppin' in to claim His Name.
Knowing that you're one with Him,
You're steppin' out and steppin' in.

Steppin' out of feeling wrong
And steppin' in, you do belong.
Steppin' out, give up the fight;
And steppin' in, you are alright.

You're listening now to what He says;
You no longer fear or have to dread.
You're steppin' out from where you've been,
Steppin' in to His Life within.

You're steppin' out of lies you've heard,
And steppin' in to believe His Word.
Steppin' out, no longer stressed,
Steppin' in to trust and rest.

"He came and preached peace to you who were far away and peace to those who were near. For through him we both have access to the Father by one Spirit." Ephesians 2:17-18 (NIV)

"The Lord is my shepherd; I have all that I need. He lets me rest in green meadows; he leads me beside peaceful streams. He renews my strength. He guides me along the right paths, bringing honor to his name." Psalms 23:1-3 (NLT)

THE HOUR IS LATE

The battle's fierce,
So much at stake,
So choose to walk
And take your place.

He's using you;
You are on the one.
Lean into Him
When you're undone.

Just take your stand;
Don't hesitate.
He needs you now;
The hour is late.

You are His choice
To be His voice,
So speak it loud
Above the crowd.

Believe His Word;
It must be heard.
You have His power,
So do not cower.

Maybe morning,
Maybe noon.
The Son of Man,
He's coming soon!

"You, dear children, are from God and have overcome them, because the one who is in you is greater than the one who is in the world." 1 John 4:4 (NIV)

"Look, I am coming soon! My reward is with me, and I will give to each person according to what they have done. I am the Alpha and the Omega, the First and the Last, the Beginning and the End." Revelation 22:12-13 (NIV)

TRADITIONS OF MEN

Walk out of the past,
And step into the new.
Those traditions of men
That you've always clung to,

That fit like a shoe
But felt empty inside;
Those ones handed down
That others supplied.

For this is the day
You lay them aside
And walk with the Savior;
'Cause you are His bride!

His love is for you,
And His Word is your guide.
He'll lead from within
'Cause He lives inside.

Let go of the past,
Those traditions of men,
The ones you marched to
But felt empty within.

Then the scales will fall off;
You'll see from a new lens.
New freedom you'll find
When you spend time with Him!

"See to it that there is no one who takes you captive through philosophy and empty deception in accordance with the tradition of men, in accordance with the elementary principles of the world, rather than in accordance with Christ. For in Him all the fullness of Deity dwells in bodily form, and in Him you have been made complete, and He is the head over every ruler and authority." Colossians 2:8-10 (NASB20)

TWO FOR ONE

You're wrapped in love,
A package deal.
Christ lives in you;
You have His seal!

He paid it all,
God's only Son.
He died for you;
Now two for one.

There's union now;
You're not alone.
The cross did work;
It brings you home.

Jesus is your Life;
You're one with Him.
He paid the price;
He took your sin.

Don't run ahead
But trust instead.
He'll lead within.
He calls you friend.

You'll walk and talk
And know Him more.
This two for one,
Do not ignore

Such sacrifice,
This love of Christ.
You once were dead
But now have Life!

"I am praying not only for these disciples but also for all who will ever believe in me through their message. I pray that they will all be one, just as you and I are one—as you are in me, Father, and I am in you. And may they be in us so that the world will believe you sent me." John 17:20-21 (NLT)

"For in Him all the fullness of Deity dwells in bodily form, and in Him you have been made complete, and He is the head over every ruler and authority." Colossians 2:8-10 (NASB20)

WALKING IN FAVOR

The veil has been lifted;
I'm walking anew.
I'm thinking more clearly
And believing it's true.

I'm favored; I'm loved.
I'm blessed and esteemed.
I'm valued; I'm called,
For I am redeemed!

I'm anointed in favor.
I'm blessed and made new.
I'm filled with His goodness
And always pursued.

He's opening new doors
And establishing my ways.
He's pulling down strongholds
For all of my days.

His love knows no end,
So I give Him my all.
I'm accepted; I'm blessed,
And I choose to stand tall.

His favor is endless.
His mercies are new.
Now I'm walking in favor
And lovin' the view!

"Surely, Lord, you bless the righteous; you surround them with your favor as with a shield." Psalm 5:12 (NIV)

"I keep asking that the God of our Lord Jesus Christ, the glorious Father, may give you the Spirit of wisdom and revelation, so that you may know him better. I pray that the eyes of your heart may be enlightened in order that you may know the hope to which he has called you, the riches of his glorious inheritance in his holy people, and his incomparably great power for us who believe." Ephesians 1:17-19a (NIV)

WALKING IN HIM

Come walk in My Ways,
Says the Ancient of Days.
Come sit at My feet,
For I've made you complete.

I took all your sin,
And you're now born again.
My heart beats for you,
For I've made you brand-new.

No longer will milk satisfy you.
You're now growing up,
And the meat of My Word
Will surely do.

So beware, lest you hear
And turn a deaf ear;
You'll learn to discern,
To make the right turn.

Be wise in My ways
Without delay.
Spend time with Me, child,
And sit for a while.

For I've got a plan
And will make you My voice.
I'll whisper to you
So you make the right choice.

I'm praying for you
That you can find rest
And be quick to say yes
Midst the fear and distress.

For My Word and My Presence
Will make you mature;
For I am Your Life,
So you will endure.

For I am The Builder;
I'm faithful and true—
I've overcome death,
And I did it for you!

For My glory is here,
So come walk in My ways.
I'll make your path clear
For all of Your days.

For you are unique
And part of My plan
So come walk with me, child,
I'm the Great, I AM!

> "There is much more we would like to say about this, but it is difficult to explain, especially since you are spiritually dull and don't seem to listen. You have been believers so long now that you ought to be teaching others. Instead, you need someone to teach you again the basic things about God's word. You are like babies who need milk and cannot eat solid food. For someone who lives on milk is still an infant and doesn't know how to do what is right. Solid food is for those who are mature, who through training have the skill to recognize the difference between right and wrong." Hebrews 5:11-14 (NLT)

WALKING THROUGH THE CROSS TODAY

My gentle Savior comes to me
And whispers in my ear today.
Come walk with Me; I'll pull you close.
I've much to share and much to say.

We're walking through the cross today.
My home is you; you'll be ok.
You'll know My pain; there will be scars.
Then you'll be known for Whose you are.

Your sins were nailed to that tree;
They're paid in full, and you are free.
You died with Me upon that cross.
Now you will reign and share My cause.

You'll know My works; I've chosen you.
Just yield to Me; there are so few
Who choose My ways and will obey.

Your family may not understand.
I'll take your fear; just hold My hand.
The time is now; I'm calling you.
My love will surely see you through.

You have to die; you have to shed
Those fleshly patterns, put to bed.
We'll do it daily; just you and Me
So My Spirit reigns and sets you free.

I'll pour My gifts upon you, child.
They've been dormant for a while,
But now they'll bear much fruit in you
As others know My love is true.

You'll hear My voice; you'll know it clear.
Your trust will build; I'll take your fear.
We're walking through the cross today,
So walk with Me; don't turn away.

I am the Way, the Truth, the Life
And we are one; you're sanctified.
You're set apart; just watch and pray.
We're walking through the cross today.

"For by his sacrifice he died to sin's power once and for all, but he now lives continuously for the Father's pleasure. So let it be the same way with you! Since you are now joined with him, you must continually view yourselves as dead and unresponsive to sin's appeal while living daily for God's pleasure in union with Jesus, the Anointed One." Romans 6:10-11 (TPT)

"...throw off your old sinful nature and your former way of life, which is corrupted by lust and deception. Instead, let the Spirit renew your thoughts and attitudes. Put on your new nature, created to be like God—truly righteous and holy." Ephesians 4:22-24 (NLT)

YOUR YESTERDAYS

The pain of undue shame
Loudly lingers in my mind,
Catching glimpses of my wrong
That I've rehearsed for quite some time.

Then one day without ado
Comes the rescue call to me.
Jesus speaks so very gently
And gives me sight so I can see.

I've seen your tears, He whispers,
And I've wiped them all away,
So get up and come with Me, my child,
For this is a brand new day.

No need to linger in your pain,
For it's weighed you down too long.
My heart is yours.
The past is gone;
Let's sing a brand-new song.

The fragrance of My love
Will be known where e'er we go
'Cause I've got some folk
Who cannot cope,
And you're My chosen one,
You know!

For in your time of suffering
And the hurt you've felt inside,
I'll redeem those years
And all your tears,
To gently turn the tide.

You are My choice
To be My voice,
To spread My love around.
They'll know My love
Because we're one
As we break those barriers down.

So watch Me work and yield to Me;
I've got a plan today.
Stay close to Me
'Cause others hurt
Just like your yesterdays.

> "He heals the wounds of every shattered heart." Psalm 147:3 (TPT)

> "... I press on to take hold of that for which Christ Jesus took hold of me. Brothers and sisters, I do not consider myself yet to have taken hold of it. But one thing I do: Forgetting what is behind and straining toward what is ahead, I press on toward the goal to win the prize for which God has called me heavenward in Christ Jesus." Philippians 3:12b-14 (NIV)

HIS PURPOSE

"And we know that God causes all things to work together for good to those who love God, to those who are called according to His purpose."

Romans 8:28 (NASB20)

God is God, and He works all things, including your life, according to His purposes. Nothing can happen without God ordaining it. We get to fully live in Christ and enjoy His blessings and purposes:

> "I cry out to God Most High, to God who will fulfill his purpose for me." Psalm 57:2 (NLT)

> "'For I know the plans that I have for you,' declares the Lord, 'plans for welfare and not for evil, to give you a future and a hope.'" Jeremiah 29:11 (ESV)

Believers no longer live in the flesh, since we now live in God's Spirit:

> "Those who are dominated by the sinful nature think about sinful things, but those who are controlled by the Holy Spirit think about things that please the Spirit… But you are not controlled by your sinful nature. You are controlled by the Spirit if you have the Spirit of God living in you. (And remember that those who do not have the Spirit of Christ living in them do not belong to him at all.)" Romans 8:5, 9 (NLT)

But we can still walk by those old fleshly attitudes when we are deceived. This is why we need the renewing of our minds:

> "Don't copy the behavior and customs of this world, but let God transform you into a new person by changing the way you think. Then you will learn to know God's will for you, which is good and pleasing and perfect." Romans 12:2 (NLT)

The deeds of the flesh are all listed in Galatians 5:17–21. The fruit of the Spirit is listed in Galatians 5:22. Take some time to read these passages to see the differences.

> "If we live by the Spirit, let us keep in step with the Spirit." Galatians 5:25 (ESV)

A DELICIOUS DISH

A baking dish
Is laid out flat.
It's needing this
And needing that.

What will I fill
My day with, Lord?
What goes inside?
What to ignore?

Will I mix it with
A cup of greed?
A dash of slander?
A pinch of deceit?

Or will I choose
To humbly bow
And believe my heart
Was changed somehow?

Those days are gone
Since You came in
And new desires
Were placed within.

A cup of kindness,
Some patience, too;
A few sprigs of peace
Will surely do!

Taste buds have changed;
You've rearranged.
New freedom found;
Now love abounds.

I'm one with You;
You've made me new,
A delicious dish
I now can chew.

No need to munch
On fleshly stuff
'Cause now I know
You are enough.

So help me, Lord,
To know Your will
And choose
Your ingredients
So they will spill

On others' lives
That need revived
So they will know
You satisfy!

REFLECTIONS AFTER A BROADCAST FROM DAILYAUDIOBIBLE.COM

"But now you must also rid yourselves of all such things as these: anger, rage, malice, slander, and filthy language from your lips. Do not lie to each other, since you have taken off your old self with its practices and have put on the new self, which is being renewed in knowledge in the image of its Creator." Colossians 3:8-10 (NIV)

DISTRACTIONS

The enemy distracts.
Oh, he's so very good at that!
You make plans to fight the war
With the One you so adore.

Then right behind your plans—
To sit down with the Son of Man—
Comes that sly, deceptive roar
Of all those pressing household chores.

So now your choice is clear
To drive the enemy out of here.
Seek first His Kingdom come;
Then the battle will be won.

As you turn to seek His face,
All else will fall in place.
When you choose to put Him first,
The enemy's plans He will reverse.

You'll know His will for you,
And His love will see you through.
So choose His loving voice
Above that harassing, inner noise.

Then His purpose will unfold,
And His Glory you'll behold.
As you learn to sing His praise,
You'll be His vessel all your days!

"But seek first his kingdom and his righteousness, and all these things will be given to you as well." Matthew 6:33 (NIV)

"Since, then, you have been raised with Christ, set your hearts on things above, where Christ is, seated at the right hand of God. Set your minds on things above, not on earthly things. For you died, and your life is now hidden with Christ in God. When Christ, who is your life, appears, then you also will appear with him in glory." Colossians 3:1-4 (NIV)

A FORK IN THE ROAD

A fork in the road—
Which path will I choose?
A decision to make—
Two roads are in view.

Pleasure or purpose.
Which road do I take?
As time is now fading
And just what is at stake?

The way of the cross,
Oh, what will it cost?
Will I choose my own way
Or suffer the loss?

Pleasure or purpose,
Doubt or belief?
Walking with Jesus
Or all about me?

Wanting His will
And His perfect design,
Or will I walk in the flesh
And leave Jesus behind?

A decision each day—
That fork in the road.
Which path will I take—
What can I afford?

Will I choose Us together
Or go my own way?
Will I trust Us together
Or do what I say?

Am I wanting His will
But pulled by my own,
For the flesh wants its way
In its own comfort zone.

My walk will depend
On what I believe—
If I need to help Jesus,
Then I'm surely deceived.

For you see, I am One
There's Life found in Him.
I'm One with the Master
And He'll lead from within.

Will I share in His sufferings
And believe He's my Life?
Will I want to know Him
And believe I'm His bride?

Will I want to know Him
And really believe?
He's my very best friend,
And He's living in me?

> "So I say, let the Holy Spirit guide your lives. Then you won't be doing what your sinful nature craves. The sinful nature wants to do evil, which is just the opposite of what the Spirit wants. And the Spirit gives us desires that are the opposite of what the sinful nature desires. These two forces are constantly fighting each other, so you are not free to carry out your good intentions." Galatians 5:16-17 (NLT)

> "Yet all of the accomplishments that I once took credit for, I've now forsaken them and I regard it all as nothing compared to the delight of experiencing Jesus Christ as my Lord! To truly know him meant letting go of everything from my past and throwing all my boasting on the garbage heap. It's all like a pile of manure to me now, so that I may be enriched in the reality of knowing Jesus Christ and embrace him as Lord in all of his greatness. My passion is to be consumed with him and not cling to my own 'righteousness' based in keeping the written Law. My only 'righteousness' will be his, based on the faithfulness of Jesus Christ—the very righteousness that comes from God." Philippians 3:7-9 (TPT)

A HOUSE CALL

Your Word is my anchor;
Your promises, my hope.
My joy is in You;
You help me to cope.

You encourage my heart
When hope starts to wane.
When the darkness seems real,
You help me push through
Or start over again.

You complete what You start
With a purpose so clear;
You cheer me on
And take all my fear.

Jesus, my friend,
Oh, the Ancient of Days,
With my voice I will raise
For all of my days.

I'm only one voice,
But this is my choice.
You've brought heaven to earth
When You gave me new birth.

Oh, how could it be
That the Ruler of All
Could choose to find me
And make a house call?

But the best news all day
Is that You've chosen to stay
In my heart for forever
And forever, always!

"I kept looking until thrones were set up, and the Ancient of Days took His seat..." Daniel 7:9 (NASB20)

"No one can come to me unless the Father who sent me draws them to me, and at the last day I will raise them up." John 6:44 (NLT)

"For the Son of Man came to seek and to save the lost." Luke 19:10 (NIV)

A WAITING FAITH

Trust God in the waiting;
He's not made a mistake.
You've done all you can,
So trust Him today.

The promise will come,
So simply succumb
And leave what you've done
In the hands of the Son.

He remembers the deed,
So trust and believe.
The promise still stands
With the reward yet at hand.

Just wait for the promise
Like the saints did of old.
They'll all be rewarded
Just like they've been told.

Oh, His timing is best,
So trust and just rest;
Though left unresolved,
He will fix and resolve.

The promise will come
But just not today.
He's just looking for faith
In the midst of the wait.

"And without faith it is impossible to please God, because anyone who comes to him must believe that he exists and that he rewards those who earnestly seek him." Hebrews 11:6 (NIV)

"And all these, though commended through their faith, did not receive what was promised, since God had provided something better for us, that apart from us they should not be made perfect." Hebrews 11:39-40 (ESV)

ARE YOU WILLING?

Are you willing to lay it down, my child,
    And trust My plans for you,
And know there's nothing left to do,
    Though rewards seem sometimes few?

Are you willing to suffer pain and loss
    And share in all I do
And bear the pain and suffering, child,
    Just like I did for you?

Are you willing to suffer silently
    And lay it down by Me
And trust My best and do with less,
    Instead of vanity?

Are you willing to bear My cross with Me
    And share in things unseen,
Or go your way and love the world
    With all its pomp and bling?

Are you willing, child, to lean on Me,
    And share My agony,
And wait awhile and rest in grace
    And share My victory?

Are you willing, child, to bear My Name
    And walk this way with Me,
Or go your way, and love the world
    And miss out on unity?

Are you truly willing to bear My Name
    And walk with Me alone,
To hear My voice above the noise
    And know Me as your own?

"And he said to all, 'If anyone would come after me, let him deny himself and take up his cross daily and follow me. For whoever would save his life will lose it, but whoever loses his life for my sake will save it." Luke 9:23-24 (ESV)

"that I may know Him and the power of His resurrection and the fellowship of His sufferings, being conformed to His death; if somehow I may attain to the resurrection from the dead." Philippians 3:10-11 (NASB20)

COME GO WITH ME

Mark My words
And be My voice.
I love you so.
You are my choice.

I've chosen you.
You're set apart.
You hear me well;
You know my heart.

So listen well;
Stay tuned to Me.
So much to say
Without delay.

A brand new work
I have for you.
Lean into Me;
Sit on My knee.

My abiding love
Has healed your wounds.
My light shines through;
You were made new.

So take My hand.
We've much to do.
Come go with Me.
Just Me and you!

"You whom I have taken from the ends of the earth and called from its remotest parts, and said to you, 'You are My servant, I have chosen you and have not rejected you.'" Isaiah 41:9 (NASB20)

"'You are My witnesses,' declares the Lord, 'and My servant whom I have chosen, that you may know and believe me and understand that I am he. Before me no god formed, nor shall there be any after Me.'" Isaiah 43:10 (ESV)

CRUCIFIED WITH CHRIST

Stepping in His steps
And walking in His ways.
You've been called upon
To be a friend and
Share her darkened days.

You've been crucified with Christ
And said yes to what He asked.
He led you down some rough terrain;
You said yes to His hard task.

You've been present in the moment
And have shed His love anew.
You've heard His voice;
You've gone when sent, and
His strength has seen you through.

You've been crucified with Christ
And came to meet a need.
You did not run or turn away,
And you planted lots of seeds.

You listened well;
You gave her hope
As she needed to be heard.
You shared His love
When called upon—
Sometimes without a word.

You've been crucified with Christ
And have chosen love and grace,
Just like the Savior did for you
When He died and took your place.

"I have been crucified with Christ. It is no longer I who live, but Christ who lives in me. And the life which I now live in the flesh I live by faith in the Son of God, who loved me and gave Himself up for me." Galatians 2:20 (ESV)

DIVINELY PLACED

The sun is up
In view today.
We're reminded, Lord,
That You did say

You are the Light;
You are the Way.
You've given us
A brand new day
To chase the darkness
Far away.

You place us out
In front each day
To be your signs,
To light the way.

You've plugged us in;
We are Your light.
We have Your love,
So we'll shine brightly
In the night.

We are Your bulbs,
Your neon signs,
Divinely placed
So others find

The joy we know—
The Risen Christ,
Who died for us
So long ago!

Divinely placed,
Strategically planned
To be His feet,
To be His hands.

To scatter us
Throughout the globe—
To light the way
And spread His hope!

Reflections after a Mike Q. Daniel teaching

"You are the light of the world—like a city on a hilltop that cannot be hidden. No one lights a lamp and then puts it under a basket. Instead, a lamp is placed on a stand, where it gives light to everyone in the house. In the same way, let your good deeds shine out for all to see, so that everyone will praise your heavenly Father." Matthew 5:14-16 (NLT)

DO NOT LOSE HEART

Do not lose heart
Or be disgraced
When He chose you
To run the race.

What you did—
Just leave it there.
He used you, child—
You're quite a pair!

A chosen vessel,
A friend to Him,
Go to the gym
Or take a swim.

Don't mull it over
Or second guess
But trust His work—
He knows what's best.

Do not lose heart—
You served Him well.
You've gone when sent—
You went to tell

Of His great love.
You've borne much fruit,
So lay it down—
He'll change your mood.

Just leave what's done
And don't succumb
To the enemy's voice—
You have a choice.

Just trust His work
He did through you
That He will use
For one or two.

Do not lose heart;
You're one with Him.
He loves you so—
He calls you friend.

You served Him well—
You heard from Him.
You gave your yes—
Now trust and rest!

"We now have this light shining in our hearts, but we ourselves are like fragile clay jars containing this great treasure. This makes it clear that our great power is from God, not from ourselves. We are pressed on every side by troubles, but we are not crushed. We are perplexed, but not driven to despair. We are hunted down, but never abandoned by God. We get knocked down, but we are not destroyed. Through suffering, our bodies continue to share in the death of Jesus so that the life of Jesus may also be seen in our bodies. Yes, we live under constant danger of death because we serve Jesus, so that the life of Jesus will be evident in our dying bodies. So we live in the face of death, but this has resulted in eternal life for you." 2 Corinthians 4:7-12 (NLT)

GET IN THE GAME

Days are evil.
Stay alert.
He's searched and searched
Throughout the earth.

He's calling you;
He knows your name.
You are His son;
Get in the game.

Listen closely
For His voice.
He'll pray through you;
You are His choice.

Evil marches all around.
It's now the time
To heed the sound.

His voice is clear;
He needs you now.
Stand in the gap
And humbly bow.

A battle cry
He's sounding forth.
Too much at stake
To lie and wait.

The souls of men,
They need set free.
The battle's won
Down on your knees.

So heed His call.
It's time to pray.
Get in the game;
Do it today!

"The next morning, Jesus got up long before daylight, left the house while it was dark, and made his way to a secluded place to give himself to prayer." Mark 1:35 (TPT)

"This is the confidence we have in approaching God: that if we ask anything according to his will, he hears us. And if we know that he hears us—whatever we ask—we know that we have what we have asked of Him." 1 John 5:14-15 (NIV)

HARVEST TIME

Seeds were sown
Way back when
And scattered out
Amongst the wind.

Some took root,
And some did not,
And others fell
Beneath the rock.

But now is here.
It's harvest time.
You're set apart,
And you are mine.

You've borne much fruit;
You've gone when sent.
You've been with Me;
You are My friend.

Though you can't see
Just what we've done
Together, you and I,
We're one.

A hundredfold,
It's harvest time.
My faithful one,
Let me remind

You that you're loved
Straight from above.
You labored then
'Cause you were sent.

My Word's gone out;
You've heard My voice.
You listened well;
It was your choice.

So look around;
A glimpse you'll see.
You've made Me known;
Now they know Me!

"Still other seed fell on good soil, where it produced a crop—a hundred, sixty or thirty times what was sown. Whoever has ears, let him hear." Matthew 13:8-9 (NIV)

"'You are My witnesses,' declares the Lord, 'and my servant whom I have chosen, so that you may know and believe me and understand that I am he.'" Isaiah 43:10a

HIGHER THINGS

Peering through a barren ground
High atop a mountain range,
A fragile, gentle wildflower
Emerges without fame.

No one cares
This flower is there;
No sounds are made or heard.
And traveling there
Is never good;
It seems to be absurd.

But God created
This lovely flower
To glorify His Name.
It's planted high
Up near the sky
And called to
Higher things.

And so it is with you as well:
You're created for His will.
And where He plants you,
It's up to Him,
And His purposes,
He will fulfill.

For what you do
When no one sees
God will one day reward
'Cause He sent His Son
Who died alone;
His blood He could afford.

He paid the price
For all your sin
And nailed them to a tree,
And now you have a choice as well;
He'll give you liberty!

You'll soar with Him
On eagle's wings
When He calls you
Close to Him.

He'll set you apart
From all the rest,
And you'll fellowship within.

Sometimes your friends won't understand.
They'll mock and laugh at you,
But just remember you're called to Him.
His joy will see you through.

So trust His heart
And take His hand
And believe He knows what's best.
For He's chosen you for higher things
And to rest upon His chest.

> "Since you have been raised to new life with Christ, set your sights on the realities of heaven, where Christ sits in the place of honor at God's right hand. Think about the things of heaven, not the things of earth. For you died to this life, and your real life is hidden with Christ in God. And when Christ, who is your life, is revealed to the whole world, you will share in all his glory." Colossians 3:1-4 (NLT)

LETTING GO

That friend of yours
For many a year,
That one you love
That you hold dear:

You must let go;
Her time is near.
I'm calling her,
So do not fear.

This is the hour;
This is the day,
So just let go;
She cannot stay.

I need her now;
Her home awaits.
I'll walk her through
Those pearly gates.

You'll meet again;
It won't be long.
So let her go;
Just sing My songs.

One day soon
You'll meet again.
You'll see her face;
You'll call her friend.

Oh, she'll be there
With no restraints.
Her seat's reserved
With all the saints.

That Banquet Table
That you'll be at,
Look down that row
'Cause she'll see you
And smile right back!

"And when the hour came, he reclined at table, and the apostles with him. And he said to them, 'I have earnestly desired to eat this Passover with you before I suffer. For I tell you I will not eat it until it is fulfilled in the kingdom of God.'" Luke 22:14-16 (ESV)

"'Let us be glad and rejoice, and let us give honor to him. For the time has come for the wedding feast of the Lamb, and his bride has prepared herself. She has been given the finest of pure white linen to wear.' For the fine linen represents the good deeds of God's holy people. And the angel said to me, 'Write this: Blessed are those who are invited to the wedding feast of the Lamb.' And he added, 'There are true words that come from God.'" Revelation 19:7-9 (NLT)

LISTEN UP

Listen up:
The time is near.
So many lost
And filled with fear.

Listen up:
The day is new.
He's coming soon;
We are His crew.

It's me and you,
His called out ones,
That hear His voice,
That know His Son.

Listen up:
The church must hear,
That remnant who
Will just draw near.

He's coming soon;
He's made that clear.
His Word is true,
So do not fear.

Listen up:
The time is now
To plant the seeds
So they will sprout.

Get in the game
And fish for men.
So many lost
Away from Him.

Remember back,
Remember when,
When He came in
And took your sin.

We are His sheep;
We know His call.
We follow Him
Above it all.

His love's the same
Throughout the earth.
So many need
A second birth.

So listen up
And be that one
Who shares God's love,
Who knows His Son!

> "My sheep listen to my voice; I know them, and they follow me." John 10:27 (NLT)

> "As has just been said: 'Today, if you hear his voice, do not harden your hearts as you did in the rebellion.'" Hebrews 3:15 (NIV)

MY GLORY DAYS

Come sit with Me, my child,
And ponder in My ways.
Come let Me share My love
As your lips pour forth My praise.

Oh, chosen one of mine,
Stand tall and walk with Me.
For My plans will soon unfold,
So trust and just believe.

Yesterday is gone,
And in the now,
You do belong.
Let go of guilt and shame
And stay clinging to My Name.

The union that we share
No one could e'er compare.
The best is yet to come,
For we've only just begun.

You're My remnant in this day
Before the Church is caught away,
And My Glory will be known
Throughout the earth
And right in homes.

My plans will flow through you,
So stay alert in all you do.
This is My final hour,
And I've given you My power!

So let My Glory flow,
And with My promptings
You will know
That the harvest time is here
As you respond with heart and ear.

For I am coming soon.
Maybe morning,
Maybe noon,
But My Glory Days are here
Right before I do appear!

"And we all, with unveiled face, beholding the glory of the Lord, are being transformed into the same image from one degree of glory to another. For this comes from the Lord who is the Spirit." 2 Corinthians 3:18 (ESV)

"So I am willing to endure anything if it will bring salvation and eternal glory in Christ Jesus to those God has chosen." 2 Timothy 2:10 (NLT)

REMEMBER

Reflect on My goodness;
Reflect on My love.
Remember the valleys;
Remember My love.

Remember My friendship
As we walked hand in hand.
Remember the joy
When you've taken a stand.

You've listened to Me,
And you've stood in the gap.
You've poured out your heart
As you sat on My lap.

You've become My friend;
You've walked in My ways.
You've gone where I've sent,
And you've loudly proclaimed

That I am the One who sets
Your heart free,
And now our sweet union
Will witness of Me!

I am gentle
And humble
And lowly of heart.
We've labored together
Right from the start.

So rest in My love
With sweet victory.
Much fruit will be borne
Out of union with Me!

"Come to me, all you who are weary and burdened, and I will give you rest. Take my yoke upon you and learn from me, for I am gentle and humble in heart, and you will find rest for your souls. For my yoke is easy and my burden is light." Matthew 11:28-30 (NIV)

"I am praying not only for these disciples but also for all who will ever believe in me through their message. I pray that they will all be one, just as you and I are one—as you are in me, Father, and I am in you. And may they be in us so that the world will believe you sent me." John 17:20-21 (NLT)

SILENT SEASONS

Life's on hold, and silence reigns.
An anxious heart that's locked in chains.
The days seem long; you've suffered much.
Your hopes were dashed; your heart's been crushed.

The planting's done; the seeds were sown.
The days seem long; you feel alone.
You heard His voice with heart and ear.
You listened well and shed a tear.

You've seen no fruit upon the vine.
Your dreams were tossed; you've seen no sign.
You've heard His call and did obey;
You've gone when sent without delay.

Though silence reigns, you must let go.
You will not reap unless you sow.
The seeds were sown; the sun must shine.
They will bear fruit, but in His time.

So lean on Him; just trust and wait
And pray others' hearts won't hesitate
To come to Him and find His Life
And know of His great sacrifice.

But what's for certain and surely will
Is you can rest and wait until
His time is right, so just believe—
You'll reap one day with certainty!

"So let's not get tired of doing what is good. At just the right time we will reap a harvest of blessing if we don't give up." Galatians 6:9 (NLT)

"Truly, truly, I say to you, unless a grain of wheat falls into the earth and dies, it remains alone; but if it dies, it bears much fruit. Whoever loves his life loses it, and whoever hates his life in this world will keep it for eternal life." John 12:24-25 (ESV)

SUNDAY'S COMIN'

Hopes and dreams
Tossed to and fro,
Buried deep;
Where did they go?

You heard His voice;
You know it's so.
But why so long?
You want to know.

Just could it be
He has a plan,
A different day,
A certain span

Of time arranged
Not known to man
Where unexpected hope
Bursts forth,
The appointed time
With His reward.

And just like He said
So long ago,
He rearranged so
You would know

His will for you
Is right on time
And in the way
He has designed.

'Cause Sunday's comin',
New hopes arise
Like when a kid
Sees Santa's eyes.

You may or may
Not understand
Just why so long
Was in His plan,

But know one thing
Right from the start:
Just take His hand
And trust His heart.

> "...At the right time, I, the Lord, will make it happen." Isaiah 60:22 (NLT)

> "But when the fullness of the time had come, God sent forth His Son, born of a woman, born under the law, to redeem those who were under the law, so that we might receive the adoption as sons." Galatians 4:4-5 (ESV)

> "And I am sure of this, that he who began a good work in you will bring it to completion at the day of Jesus Christ." Philippians 1:6 (ESV)

THE STING OF DEATH

Always there
Remembering back,
That dread of death,
It was a fact.

When will I die,
Where will I go?
That emptiness
That gripped my soul.

But such good news
Was what we heard.
Jesus had to die,
Which seemed absurd.

He tasted death
Once and for all.
He died for us;
He took the fall.

He paid the debt
Which we all owed
And rose again
To pave the road

So we'd find Life
In Him alone and
Share the news
And be so bold.

He did it once.
It was enough
For all mankind
Out of such love.

He became sin
So we'd know Him
Then we'd repent
And be born again.

We no longer have to
Fear that day
For He took the
Sting of death away!

"'O death, where is your victory? O death, where is your sting?' The sting of death is sin, and the power of sin is the law. But thanks be to God, who gives us the victory through our Lord Jesus Christ." 1 Corinthians 15:55-57 (ESV)

THIS ONE THING

This one thing
I want to know:
To know God's Son
Above it all.

He is the Way,
The Truth, the Life;
To walk In Him,
He satisfies.

This one thing,
I'm safe in Him
When faced to
Climb out on a limb.

To share in His death
And in His life;
To walk life's path
As His dear bride.

This one thing,
Above it all:
To know God's Son
And stand up tall!

To know Him more
Above the noise,
To listen closely
For His voice.

To let Him lead
Who is the Way
So I won't walk
Another way.

"One thing I have asked of the Lord, that I will seek after: that I may dwell in the house of the Lord all the days of my life, to gaze upon the beauty of the Lord and to inquire in his temple." Psalm 27:4 (ESV)

"For you have died, and your life is hidden with Christ in God. When Christ who is your life appears, then you also will appear with Him in glory." Colossians 3:3-4 (ESV)

"And I continually long to know the wonders of Jesus and to experience the overflowing power of his resurrection working in me. I will be one with him in his sufferings and become like him in his death. Only then will I be able to experience complete oneness with him in his resurrection from the realm of death." Philippians 3:10-11 (TPT)

TIME TO LET GO

Nothing is lacking—
Those are lies from the pit.
The truth is you're enough;
You're complete, and you fit

Into His plans
And purpose for you.
You just have to know Him,
And you certainly do!

It's time now to walk
And trust Him alone.
It's time to let go
And not fear the unknown.

He's gone before you
'Cause He is the Way,
And He is your Life
For all of your days.

Your job is to focus
On Him and not you,
To trust His sure footing
In all that you do.

No need to outsmart
The enemy's demands,
But lean into Jesus
For His will and His plans.

He's filled up your lack
And made you complete.
So time to let go
Of those lies of defeat.

Just believe He knows best;
So trust and just rest,
And let go and let God
And do not second guess.

REFLECTIONS AFTER A MIKE Q. DANIEL TEACHING

"...fixing our eyes on Jesus, the pioneer and perfecter of faith. For the joy set before him endured the cross, scorning its shame, and has sat down at the right hand of the throne of God." Hebrews 12:2 (NIV)

"'For my thoughts are not your thoughts, neither are your ways my ways,' declares the Lord. 'For as the heavens are higher than the earth, so are my ways higher than your ways and my thoughts than your thoughts." Isaiah 55:8-9 (ESV)

TWO CONTRASTING KINGDOMS

Walking in newness and carrying His flame,
You have a new heart and possess a new Name.
The Word is your guide as you walk in His ways,
But you're faced with two kingdoms for all of your days.

The Kingdom of God or the Kingdom of the World?
Two contrasting kingdoms will make your head swirl.
Which path will you choose, and which way will you go?
Will you choose to lean in and just let His love flow
Or let pride be your guide and let flesh rule the show?

Christ lives in you, and you live in Him,
For He died in your place and took all your sin.
His Kingdom has come, and you carry His flame.
Your wants were made new, and you'll not be the same.

Oh, these contrasting Kingdoms will be shoved in your face,
But you have a new heart for all of your days.
As you lean into Him and He becomes great,
He'll call you to serve, and you won't always take.

Walking in darkness or choosing the light?
Letting Him lead or being denied
Of all that He has for you in this life?
Will you yield to His lead or fight to be right?

For Jesus was humble and servant to all
He died in your place because of the fall.
The power of the sword or the power of cross?
Will you demand to be right, or will you choose to take loss?

For you'll now walk by faith and not by your sight,
So spend time in His Word, and He'll lead, and He'll guide.
Then you'll learn to discern and walk in His ways
And choose the right Kingdom for all of your days!

"For all that is in the world—the desires of the flesh and the desires of the eyes and pride of life—is not from the Father but is from the world." 1 John 2:16 (ESV)

"...the kingdom of God is already among you." Luke 17:21b (NLT)

UNTIL THEN

Until then,
When all seems lost,
Help me to trust
And count the cost.

Until then,
When fears resound
And my heart breaks—
Where death abounds.

Until then,
Help me to know
You are My Life
Where e'er I go.

Until then,
Your favor rests;
I'll trust Your lead
'Cause you know best.

Until then,
You return for me.
Your grace abounds—
My guarantee.

Until then,
My source is You.
Not this life—
I'm passing through.

Until then,
This earth I'll roam—
Until you choose
To call me home.

"For the sin of this one man, Adam, caused death to rule over many. But even greater is God's wonderful grace and his gift of righteousness, for all who receive it will live in triumph over sin and death through this one man, Jesus Christ." Romans 5:17 (NLT)

"Jesus said to them, 'My food is to do the will of him who sent me and to accomplish his work. Do you not say, "There are yet four months, then comes the harvest"? Look, I tell you, lift up your eyes, and see that the fields are white for harvest.'" John 4:34-35 (ESV)

WASHING DIRTY FEET

Such a humble task
When called upon to ask
If you would serve another
And sit beneath your brother.

'Cause serving Christ our Savior
Means menial behavior
For the limelight is not there,
And no one may know you care.

But the highest price you'll pay
Is to sacrifice your day;
To wash those dirty feet
Then rinse, then wash—
Repeat.

No one may see your service,
And you doubt if there's a purpose
To sit amongst the people,
The lowly and the feeble.

But the One who really cares
Is the One who called you there.
He left heaven's glory
So you could tell His story

Of the sacrifice He made.
He took your sins and paid
All of them that day
To give His love away.

Jesus hung amongst the lowly,
The Son of God, who is most holy.
He paid the price for sin
And served you to the end.
He died and rose again,
And now He calls you friend.

So washing dirty feet
Then rinse, then wash—
Repeat,
Demonstrates His perfect love
When you serve and sit beneath.

> "So if I'm your teacher and lord and have just washed your dirty feet, then you should follow the example that I've set for you and wash one another's dirty feet. Now do for each other what I have done for you. I speak to you timeless truth: a servant is not superior to his master, and an apostle is never greater than the one who sent him." John 13:14-16 (TPT)

YOUR CALLING IS CALLING

Walking in comfort for many a day
Has been His will as you've walked in His ways,
But He's blowing the winds and the waves by the sea
And causing discomfort with no guarantee.

Oh, He's stirring you up with new focus in view
'Cause He has a new work and a calling on you.
Far out in the distance from the land and the shore
Peers a mountaintop range no one can ignore.

He now says it is time; you are ready for more—
You were born to fly and not stay on the shore.
Your purpose is clear, for this is the year
To soar like an eagle, so give Him your fears.

He's causing discomfort so you'll leave the nest—
So you will trust Him and believe He knows best.
He's chosen you, child; you were hand-picked by Him—
For now is the time to soar on the wind!

Oh, the Ancient of Days has planned out your ways,
And His Glory will rest and shine upon you
As you leave all behind and come follow the new!

"But those who trust in the LORD will find new strength. They will soar high on wings like eagles. They will run and not grow weary. They will walk and not faint." Isaiah 40:31 (NLT)

I don't depend on my own strength to accomplish this; however I do have one compelling focus: I forget all of the past as I fasten my heart to the future instead. I run straight for the divine invitation of reaching the heavenly goal and gaining the victory-prize through the anointing of Jesus." Philippians 3:13-14 (TPT)

YOUR INHERITANCE

He had you in mind
When He died on that cross.
He loved you back then
With all of your flaws.

But He made a way
To redeem and make new
At the time He was dying
And thinking about you.

You're valued; you're loved.
Jesus took all your sin.
You were bought with a price,
And you're now born again!

You've an inheritance so sure
That will not fade away—
Your reservation is kept
For that glorious day!

Oh, He keeps His Word
With a sure guarantee,
And His promises are true—
Meant to set your heart free.

His purpose is you,
And it's you He pursues.
Your inheritance is free
'Cause His blood paid your dues.

He is the path
Because He is the Way,
And His deepest desire
Is to share all your days.

A joint heir with Jesus—
Oh yes, it is true!
God gifted His love
And sent Jesus to you!

Reflections after a message by Tim Chalas

"In him we have obtained an inheritance, having been predestined according to the purpose of him who works all things according to the counsel of his will." Ephesians 1:11 (ESV)

"But he said to me, 'My grace is sufficient for you, for my power is made perfect in weakness.' Therefore I will boast all the more gladly about my weaknesses, so that Christ's power may rest on me."

2 Corinthians 12:9 (NIV)

ACKNOWLEDGEMENTS

Thanks go to Beth and Gary Suess and the team of Kingdom Winds for publishing my new book, *Walking in Favor, Stepping into Grace*. I especially want to thank Codi Ribitzki with Kingdom Winds for her expertise, advice, and creativity in producing such a beautiful layout of this new book as well as *All My Desire*!

Thank you to my friends, Sharon Hyatt, Sandy Wilhite, Debbie Smith, Joan King, Naomi Krstinic, Betty McBride, and my sister, Linda Amos, for their help, wisdom, and prayers throughout the writing process. I also want to thank all my writer friends that have been with me on zoom calls. What a tremendous blessing and encouragement each of you has been to me. Thank you for your love and great sacrifice!

And thank you to Carol Krum, Naomi Krstinic, Debbie Andrews Smith, Sharon Hyatt, Debi Finklea, Betty McBride, and Kim Rees who took the time to write an endorsement in the front of the book!

A "shout out" goes to Priscilla Shirer, Graham Cooke, Frank Friedmann, and Tim Chalas for their words I quoted to further clarify

what favor and grace mean in our Christian walk. I also want to thank Mike Daniel, Frank Friedmann, Tim Chalas, Graham Cooke, Daily Audio Bible, and Rick Atchley for their encouraging messages that the Lord used in my life to inspire some of my writings.

Also, I want to thank my friend, Rainy Mitchell. Rainy was the one God used in my life to suggest I write a poetry book in 2019. Rainy helped me accomplish that task by writing my first book, *Come and Sit With Me Awhile*. With the help of Allen Joanis with Ketos Creative LLC, Rainy turned some of my poetry into songs, which are on an album called, "Revelation" with Rainy Mitchell. You can find it on Spotify, YouTube, etc.

And to my husband, Ron, who has been my biggest supporter since Day 1 when God called me into writing Christian poetry in 2003: I certainly could never have fulfilled this God-given dream without your love, encouragement, and help along the way.

The Lord truly gets all the glory for what He has done in and through me. Without a doubt, my Jesus gets sweeter as the years go by. What a Savior; what a friend!

www.ingramcontent.com/pod-product-compliance
Lightning Source LLC
Chambersburg PA
CBHW072151070526
44585CB00015B/1090